MW00791967

DEEMER
ON
TECHNICAL
ANALYSIS

DEEMER

ON

TECHNICAL ANALYSIS

Expert Insights on Timing the Market and Profiting in the Long Run

WALTER DEEMER
AND SUSAN CRAGIN

New York Chicago San Francisco Lisbon London Madrid Mexico City
Milan New Delhi San Juan Seoul Singapore Sydney Toronto

The McGraw·Hill Companies

Copyright © 2012 by Walter Deemer. All rights reserved. Printed in the United States of America. Except as permitted under the United States Copyright Act of 1976, no part of this publication may be reproduced or distributed in any form or by any means, or stored in a database or retrieval system, without the prior written permission of the publisher.

1 2 3 4 5 6 7 8 9 10 DOC/DOC 1 9 8 7 6 5 4 3 2

ISBN   978-0-07-178568-6
MHID   0-07-178568-X

e-ISBN   978-0-07-178569-3
e-MHID   0-07-178569-8

Library of Congress Cataloging-in-Publication Data

Deemer, Walter
  Deemer on technical analysis : expert insights on timing the market and profiting in the long run / by Walter Deemer, Susan Cragin.
    p. cm.
  Includes index.
  ISBN-13: 978-0-07-178568-6 (alk. paper)
  ISBN-10: 0-07-178568-X (alk. paper)
    1. Technical analysis (Investment analysis)   2. Investment analysis.
    3. Portfolio management.   4. Investments.   I. Cragin, Susan.
    II. Title.
  HG4529.D44 2012
  332.63'2042—dc23   2011042437

McGraw-Hill books are available at special quantity discounts to use as premiums and sales promotions or for use in corporate training program. To contact a representative, please e-mail us at bulksales@mcgraw-hill.com.

This book is printed on acid-free paper.

from Walter
To Bobbie

from Susan
To Mark

CONTENTS

CHAPTER **25**

PREFACE

I've worked on Wall Street since I started at Merrill Lynch in 1963—and I have been a full-time technical analyst since 1964. During that time, I've been lucky enough to have worked with—and learned from—some of the best technical analysts of all time. Some of them are household names, such as Bob Farrell, but others, although they were revered in institutional circles, are virtually unknown by the general public (e.g., Stan Berge).

This book shares the lessons I've learned from the great teachers I've worked with—as well as some lessons I've learned myself through long experience. (Experience is the best teacher in the stock market, too.) The book is not, however, just another exhaustive treatise on technical analysis; others have already written them better than I ever could. Nor is it a complete book on investing. The space we had to work with was far from infinite, and difficult choices on what to include and what to leave out had to be made. But I think everyone, from seasoned professional money managers to the public investor, who deserves a lot more credit than Wall Street usually gives him or her, will find some illuminating—and, I hope, profitable—nuggets of investment wisdom in these pages.

I've been thinking about this book for a long time, and as I neared retirement, I thought that its time had finally come. I desperately needed someone to help me write it, though, and Susan Cragin, the wife of a money manager I knew through some mutual friends and a published author ("Nuclear Nebraska"), said that she'd be interested in coauthoring it. Our original title was *Don't Call It Luck*—but I was very, very lucky to have had Susan to work with; she was unceasingly cheerful and creative throughout, and without her, there would be no book.

What I Do Now

After 47 years on Wall Street, I "retired" in December 2010. But the stock market is in my blood, so I still write comments whenever I have something to say and send them to some long-term clients and friends who are kind enough to supplement my Social Security checks once in a while.

Old technicians never die; they just chart away. . . .

ACKNOWLEDGMENTS

We would like to thank our wonderful agent, John Willig of Literary Services, and Mary Glenn, Morgan Ertel, Daina Penikas, Sara Hendricksen, and Tania Loghmani, all of McGraw-Hill Professional.

Our spouses, Bobbie Deemer and Mark Ungewitter, have provided comments and suggestions, proofreading expertise, and love and support. Mark has also provided many of the charts found in this book. In addition, Ron Griess of The Chartstore.com provided us with charts specifically created for this book. Stephen Pope, June Blake, and Penny Wolfe provided invaluable comments and proofreading. Wine HQ provided computer support and Diane Gallagher provided Walter's photo under a very tight deadline.

In addition, Walter wishes to especially thank the people who have guided and encouraged him throughout his career and during the writing of this book. These people have all been recognised in the pages that follow. Two people deserve special mention, however: Bob Farrell, who has given me continuous guidance and support from the day I first met him right up until the present, and Dean LeBaron, who has been a constant source of ideas and encouragement. Also, the late Mike Epstein was an inspiration to all who knew him, and I wish he had lived long enough to see this book published. I would also like to thank David Keller, Mark Dibble, and Susan Berger of Fidelity's Technical Department for their generous invitations over the years to visit their legendary Chart Room and David, especially, for allowing a picture of it to appear in this book. (I had no idea how high an honor it was until I told Susan Berger about it and she responded: "Wow; they never allow pictures to be taken in there.") And above all, my wife Bobbie deserves a special mention for her loving support in this and all my other endeavors. Without her, where would I be?

INTRODUCTION

As I write this in the fall of 2011, most people feel that their savings and investments are in jeopardy. The financial markets and economy are in turmoil, unemployment and underemployment are high, our economy seems to consume but not produce, and our government's spending policies seem to have put us on an unsustainable trajectory.

Most people think that there is a solution for these problems lurking somewhere in government. They couldn't be more wrong.

Our economy is in the midst of a large structural corrective phase that is not going to end anytime soon. Our credit is tapped out, our financial sector has overspent, our government has overspent, and our consumers have overspent, and it will take an awful lot of time to correct all of the past excesses and for the economy to get back on a sound footing with the investment and savings that are needed for economic growth.

In the meantime, the stock market is in the midst of a "secular bear market," where prices go essentially sideways—at best—for well over a decade. This is a much, much harsher investment environment than we have been used to, and it means that investors are going to have to work harder and harder to get "normal" returns.

In times like these, it is up to investors to take charge of their own investments and do for themselves what their brokers or mutual funds will not do for them—and that is to time their purchases and sales to be in the market when it is rising and out when it is falling. This is because the generally sideways movement of a secular bear market is made up of big shorter-term wings in both directions, and savvy investors must know how to work them to their advantage—to time purchases and sales so as to maximize their returns.

Market timing has been demonstrated to work, but it is perceived as dangerous—good only for short-term traders or for those with an unusually high risk tolerance. But these ideas, as this book will show, are either wrong or can be overcome.

First of all, even bad market timing is better than no market timing at all.

A study by analyst Gary Fritz notes that from 1990 to May 2011, the Standard & Poor's 500 Index (S&P 500) gained 278 percent, but if you missed the 20 best weeks you'd be down 1.3 percent, the typically bad results from this type of study. What the study fails to mention, though, is that all of the worst weeks and most of the best ones occurred during cyclical downtrends. But even if your market timing efforts ended up with you being out of the market during both the 20 best weeks *and* the 20 worst weeks, you'd be up 380 percent. This is not really good market timing by anyone's standard, but it still comes out well ahead of the 278 percent gain generated by a buy-and-hold strategy. And, also, keep in mind that you don't have to buy right at the bottom and sell right at the top to be a successful market timer. Even a moderate amount of success will give you a better return than a buy-and-hold strategy.

Fritz' analysis, of course, was done at a time when the market generally was rising. But now, with the market probably destined to go basically sideways for the next few years, market timing is becoming not just the best way to make money—and to keep it after you make it—but the *only* way to do so.

During a long bear market, many small investors become discouraged and drop out. My old friend John Hammerslough, then at Kaufman Alsberg, put it like this: "In a bull market, you check the prices of your stocks every day to see how much they've gone up. In a bear market, you don't even bother to look any more."

Small investors drop out because a buy-and-hold strategy doesn't work in a long bear market, and they know it. But they don't have the confidence to market-time. I hope that this book will give them this confidence.

Throughout this book, I have put in anecdotes about the markets and my life and work. Some are funny, all are interesting, but they also serve a purpose. We've been here before. Situations do repeat themselves. New paradigms, market bubbles and crashes, recessions and depressions, and terribly long recoveries have all happened before, and all of them will happen again. In the words of my incomparable mentor, Bob Farrell, "History doesn't repeat itself exactly, but behavior does."

For nearly 50 years I have made my living using technical analysis to time the market. There has always been a good reason to do so, but now and for the next few years, I consider it an imperative.

And that's where this book comes in.

PART I

WHY TECHNICAL ANALYSIS?

CHAPTER 1

WHO IS THE "AVERAGE" INVESTOR AND WHAT'S WITH THE HANDBASKET?

The "Average" Investor

Average stock market investors today may have wealth, but most are not wealthy. Most have a 401(k) account and maybe some savings to invest, and they are worried about retirement. And why not? They know that they may need much more money in retirement than they have needed to survive thus far.

Their safety nets—Social Security and Medicare—are in danger of being reduced as our government grapples with an ever-widening deficit. And another government deficit-shrinker, monetary inflation, may halve the value of all dollars over the next 15 years.

Artificially low interest rates have kept the rates of no-risk investments such as Treasury bills and bank certificates of deposit (CDs) at unattractive levels.

Health costs are astronomical, are rising, and are a black box where a seemingly simple trip to the hospital for a couple of days, with a combined total of under an hour's supervision by a doctor, can add up to hundreds of thousands of dollars. Even with health insurance, out-of-pocket costs can be steep.

Basic living costs will only rise. Taxes, energy, and food prices are on their way up.

Most Americans own a home as their major asset, but the future value of that asset is in doubt. Home prices are still falling in many parts of the country. And, as our states grapple with declining revenues, local entities, especially schools, will attempt to make up some money through increased property taxes. This will raise monthly costs and may make the value of the average family home decline further. (This is so because most home purchasers calculate the total monthly payment to determine affordability, and that payment includes an increasingly high percentage of taxes.)

Food is expected to become more expensive. Global warming, a decrease in the underground water supply, a burgeoning world population, and increased living standards all will drive up the price of food.

Energy costs will be affected by instability in the Middle Eastern and African oil-producing countries and new worries about atomic energy stemming from the recent disaster in Japan.

The formula that the government uses to tackle these problems, the "core" *consumer price index* (CPI), is flawed because it doesn't take into account the cost of energy or the cost of food. And those prices may rise the fastest.

So I Get A Part-Time Job?

It won't be easy.

Our real unemployment and underemployment rates together are near 25 percent.

Our government's unemployment figures are narrowly defined and do not include those who have given up looking or have taken part-time employment. They do not include those who have been laid off from a well-paid job and have had to make real sacrifices to feed their families by moving, retraining, and/or taking a much lower salary. They do not include young people who are unable to find a first "real" job and are working part time or in minimum-wage retail and are living in their parents' basements.

Even if government numbers painted an accurate picture of the current economy, even if they reflected the real unemployment and underemployment rate and the real rate of essential consumer-good price increases, what can the government do? Our government is so far in debt that it has run out of powder.

Our economy needs to create well-paid jobs on an unprecedented scale. But where?

Private-sector job creation used to be in vital and necessary areas such as construction, factory work, and agriculture. But the construction industry is a mess, we don't manufacture consumer disposables in the United States any more, we don't manufacture most consumer durables, and farms now hire machines, not people. In suburban America, those jobs have been replaced by nonvital jobs that depend on disposable income and consumer choice (whether this be poor choice or not, I leave to the reader's discretion). Employment among the middle class has been concentrated around financial services and real estate development and sales. Among the working class, retail and food-service seem to employ most. But all this depends on optional local consumption, demand for which can vanish overnight.

A raft of jobs that once guaranteed a modestly paid but very permanent place in the local society—the civil service, the police and fire departments, school teaching, and nursing—are now few and competitive. Military service, formerly a fallback, is now a first career option for many working-class young people.

In fact, the benefits that these modest jobs have—good health insurance and a secure retirement—were derided a few years ago as the type of compensation only conservative, unimaginative workers desired. How ironic that those same workers now seem greedy because our health care and its attendant costs have pushed the value of those benefits to heights unimagined when most of them started working.

But even these jobs may not last. Look for angry taxpayers to demand long-term efficiencies and fewer municipal services. Look for angry voters to demand an end to government mandates that require local spending, especially in the schools and social services. Look for nervous elected officials to renegotiate union contracts.

You get the picture. There seems to be little salary income on the horizon. At least in the short term, underemployment will become the norm. And there is no quick fix out there.

Investors need to save more than they ever have, they need to start sooner, and they need to make wise investment choices. Unfortunately, most of them make the wrong choices.

The Handbasket

What Are These Wrong Choices?

Small investors used to hope for a reasonable, steady return from a diversified portfolio that included cash, stocks (which small investors usually held in mutual funds), and bonds. Diversification was the mantra. In the selection of stocks, the mantra has always been *buy and hold*. Pick a portfolio, either a mutual fund or individual stocks, and stick with it.

Investors who classify themselves as *traders* tend to trade a lot and tend to watch their stock baskets obsessively, tracking the economic news, the financial news, and the company's filings.

Both methods may bring gains. But investors are usually their own worst enemies.

Today's investors are being forced to reach too much for yield.

Stock market returns until recently have been higher than average, and people have come to depend on them. Many people now are looking for 7, 8, or 9 percent returns a year from their stock portfolios.

This is especially true of retired investors, who tend to think of the *yield*, the profit on their investments, as a fluctuating part of their retirement income. The mantra is, "I'm not going to spend down my principal." The yield becomes a necessary part of their living expenses.

During the great inflation of the 1980s, retirees were getting 15 percent on their money-market funds and thought that this was going to be something they were going to enjoy for a long, long time. But they gradually saw that return go back to more normal levels and now, unfortunately, to below-normal levels. The return on money-market funds is now negligible.

Stock market investors were deluded by the outsized returns in the stock market for years, until the unfortunate incidents of the past decade (2000–2010). So they have their retirements planned around earning 7 to 9 percent compounded, year after year.

Ray DeVoe, a financial markets historian whom I first met when he was at Spencer Trask, says that more money has been lost reaching for yield than at the point of a gun. He's right. Investors now have to take on an extraordinary amount of risk to get this "normal" 7 to 9 percent return. This is going to be a lot tougher in the future than it was in the past. Historically, a *normal* risk-free yield is inflation plus about three percentage points. Right now, risk-free and low-risk yields have shrunk to almost nothing.

Not just individuals but also professional money managers have been making the same mistake. Pension funds are in a hole; they are underwater because they are projecting 8 percent compounded returns. And no one on earth knows where they are going to get them.

Getting an increased yield always—always—involves taking on increased risk.

Some financial people will gladly tell their clients that investments yielding 7 to 9 percent can be riskless. But outsized risk-free returns are not in the cards any more, and they probably never have been. A real risk-free return is usually something like inflation plus about 3 percent.

There is no such thing as a free lunch. If something sounds too good to be true, it is. But many retired people haven't changed their concept of "too good to be true" to comport with today's reality.

Making money takes some risk. Believing that there is no risk sets an investor up for fraud.

The Federal Reserve's Manipulation of Interest Rates Has Taken Small Savers Out of Cash and Cash Equivalents

The average small investor has nowhere to put cash because interest rates have been kept too low. The banks are paying 0.5 percent on a savings account. Some financial services firms aren't able to keep cash for their customers. So an entire class of assets is moving away from deposits, savings bonds, even government debt because there is no yield. (Of course, this also affects the amount of money local banks have to lend, but that's another story.)

Right now, if you have an extra $5, you put it in the stock market. And this is artificially propping up the stock market.

Interest rates, when they start going back up, are going to have all sorts of bad consequences for everyone but small savers and local businesses. The biggest consequence, of course, is that payments on government debt will skyrocket. But if interest rates go up, as they must sooner or later, bond prices will go down. This may result in a dramatic seesaw effect in stock market prices as people move in droves to cash, which is perceived as safer. We are going into a period of fear and uncertainty in the stock market. Investors are nervous. If interest rates rise, many people may withdraw money from the market, saying, "Whoopie!" 3 percent from the bank sounds like a great deal, and it is insured by the Federal Deposit Insurance Corporation (FDIC)! A positive 3 percent return, when everything else is having a negative return, is pretty good.

So I Buy Gold and Put It under the Floorboards?

Formerly, in times of uncertain financial assets, investors would shift to hard assets, but that cycle has been broken.

There is a cycle, of indeterminate length, swinging back and forth between financial assets and real, physical assets. At times, investors favor financial assets—stocks and bonds. At other times, they favor physical assets: real estate and gold. Normally, if financial assets are unattractive, this means that physical assets are attractive. But not all physical assets are attractive now.

The classic middle-class physical asset is real estate. Well, the real estate market is a mess. It's still overpriced compared with median incomes in most of the country. And there's still a huge glut of foreclosed properties that we have to get out from under before real estate can go back up. And most middle-class people buy real estate with loans and depend on being able to meet a monthly payment. Well, interest rates are near zero now, and they are going to go up at some point or another, so monthly payments will go up. Also, local real estate taxes may have to rise substantially to cover shortfalls in municipal workers' health care and pensions, as well as the school system. As monthly payments rise, house prices will fall.

Remember, a house is primarily the place where you live. And you live there because of a job, because of a tax structure, and because of schools and other amenities. Because of uncertainties about all these things, the price point may not have settled and may not settle for a while.

Over the long run, real estate is probably a good investment, but it's got a lot of short-term problems.

Other physical assets have their own problems. Some wealthier people are going into art, gold, and various commodities. But commodities are usually lousy investments unless you actually take hold of them and deliver them later. Buying copper, for example, is out of the question for most of us because you're paying storage charges and so on.

And so, the question becomes, Where do you go? Gold is doing well, but when you buy gold, are you buying gold—or are you really selling the currency short?

So I Take My Money to a Broker, Right?

When most people look at taking on a level of manageable risk, they usually think first of talking to an investment professional, a broker.

Nowadays, most financial professionals who call themselves brokers are nothing more than asset gatherers. Their responsibility virtually stops when your money walks in the door.

Here's what the average investor should already know about the average financial professional.

Most work for some combination of base salary and commission. Commission is based usually on a combination of two factors: the total amount of assets under the broker's control and transactions fees that are generated when clients purchase or exchange certain assets. Thus the broker is incented to increase the amount of money under his control, whether or not he has the time or skills to manage all of it. He also may encourage his clients to purchase assets that result in a greater commission income to himself, such as annuities. He also may encourage them to overtrade.

In a time in the market when stock prices are declining, the amount of money under management naturally shrinks, and with it, the broker's income. It becomes important for the broker to take new assets under management. At the same time, though, if stock prices are going down, the best place to be may be in cash. Investors can do that cheaper for themselves. So the broker is likely to say that he has a formula for doing better than the market.

That broker is lying. Always. (Well, almost always.)

So I Select Some Mutual Funds and Hold onto Them, Right?

Not necessarily. This may not be a good environment for professional money managers at mutual funds.

Professional money managers live under a multiedged sword. Number one, their accounts have to go up. Number two, the accounts have to go up more than the market. Number three, the accounts have to go up more than their competitors' accounts. I have seen grown money managers weep because the stock market had a very good day and their fund was up 1 percent, but their arch rival's fund was up 1.3 percent. And so it was a terrible day for them. They had lost 0.3 percent to their competitors, even though they were up 1 percent that day. So it's a horrible thing. This is why good money managers have to have iron stomachs—the stress levels are unbelievably high. And they can measure their performance day by day, hour by hour, minute by minute so that they can see how they are doing in this never-ending race every single minute, every single hour, of every single day.

This kind of atmosphere encourages money managers to take short-term risks and very short-term profits—and use very short-term charts. But over the long term, such risk necessarily must have a downside.

There is another problem. In a down market, not all managers can move to cash. Some funds are charged with being fully invested all the time. And if they are, and if they become concerned about the market, they will buy what they think are the safest, lowest-volatility stocks they can come up with. This may be the closest to a cash equivalent they can get. Many mutual fund companies will not let their investment managers go above 5 percent cash anymore. And many pension fund managers at big corporations don't let their money managers go above 5 percent cash either. They will say, "I want you to run a fully invested growth portfolio. We have another 20 percent in small-cap value stocks, and we have another 10 percent in emerging markets. And so forth. But we want to have 20 percent of assets in a high-quality growth portfolio. Therefore, you are to be fully invested at all times. If we want to have cash, we will raise it ourselves."

So the individual funds—and the individual money managers—may have very little flexibility. There are all sorts of rules.

In the old days, money managers could go 50 percent cash with no trouble. The only risk was job risk. Now it is practically impossible for them to do this. So many money managers do very different things with their personal accounts than they do with the money they manage. It's always instructive to find out what rules they live under.

If they want cash, they have to fake it.

But Won't I Need to Take Money Out of My Account?

Yes. And that may result in another source of pressure on the stock market.

When baby boomers reach the age of 70½ years, they have to withdraw money from their IRAs and 401(k)s. This phenomenon is going to put downward price pressure on stocks for the next 20 years or more.

So Who Should Do Their Own Investing? Should I? Should Everyone?

You are the best judge of this. But, in general, more people should invest for themselves than are in fact doing so. And even those who don't wish to actively manage their own investments should follow them more closely than they do. There was a cartoon once showing a broker's office with the company motto affixed above the door:

"Working to Make Your Money Our Money."

This is an apt description of all too much of the brokerage business.

Anecdote—Fund Managers' Guidelines

John Maurice ran the Putnam Growth Fund, which was the biggest fund at Putnam when I worked there. There was a time when he was more bearish than the investment policy committee, which was comprised largely of administrators. And one day he was hauled into the boss's office. And the boss said, "You are only 75 percent invested! The guidelines, the investment policy guidelines, call for funds to be 80 to 85 percent invested. And you are a member of the policy committee. So I want you to become 80 percent invested *tout suite*." John Maurice promptly took a 5 percent position in AT&T, which in those days was the most widow-and-orphan type of stock you could imagine—it had a stable price and a steady dividend. You didn't buy it for capital appreciation.

And the boss said, "What's the idea?"

And John Maurice responded, "You told me to get 80 percent invested. You didn't tell me how." And so he went 80 percent invested as safely as he could. And, as was usually the case, John Maurice was right, and the investment policy committee was wrong.

But Mutual Funds Are Still Better
than a Broker, Right?

They can be. A mutual fund manager is looking only at one pool of money. If a broker has 30 accounts or 300 accounts, you know that she's not spending much time on each one of them.

The biggest risk to buying a mutual fund is that you are getting a pig in a poke. This is so because mutual funds attract money based on the advertised performance over the recent past, and the advertised performance is often misleading.

First, only the strong funds survive. Those with weaker track records are often merged into the stronger funds. And only the track record of the stronger fund survives. So, suddenly, a strong-looking fund according to June 2011 numbers may quintuple in size in July and be loaded with bad investments. So you invest in September and find out in October that you are in a mixed fund loaded with bad investments.

Second, size matters. A small fund can be flexible and innovative. But high performance usually attracts lots of new money. A money manager can do things with a $200 million fund that she may not be able to do if she has to manage $2 billion. She may not be able to find the investments. She may lose her flexibility. Her purchases may move the market. Or it may be too stressful for her, and she may lose her edge.

Third, funds often depend on the brilliance of a single individual, who is making judgment calls, who is exercising his intelligence and experience. If he leaves the fund for any reason, expect its performance to suffer. There is no substitute for a human brain.

But mutual funds have their uses (although every investor should avoid mutual funds that have large upfront loads and other barriers to entry and egress).

In fact, young and inexperienced investors probably should be in a good, big, diversified mutual fund, especially if they have only a little money to invest. If I could give one single piece of advice to young investors with very little money, I'd say look around for a good diversified mutual fund and start putting money into it. Money that has 40 years to grow usually grows a lot more than money that has five years to grow.

The very best way to start making a fortune is to start saving money early. We know that it's tough for a young person or couple just starting out to put away some savings—but just a little bit every week or month will pay off big when you retire. (And given all the current trends, the company you work for is going to help you less and less with retirement as time passes, and you're going to have to rely more and more on your own retirement savings when the time comes.)

Should I Use an E-Trade Account and Do My Own Investing?

Not if you follow the business model espoused by most online brokerages and track your investments day by day.

This is one of the biggest mistakes that bona fide long-term investors make: They try to track their investments day by day. "I had a good day in the market yesterday," they say. But it's what happens over the next 18 years, not what happens over the next 18 days, that counts.

The accounts of at-home traders have gotten increasingly volatile. The trading fees are low. But, of course, the discount brokerages make their money from the number of transactions. So they encourage their clients to engage in a large number of trades. And they create and issue tools that encourage short-term trading.

And short-term traders are increasingly at a disadvantage against computers.

You can't move faster than a computer. If your trading strategy involves the clicking of a mouse, it's too slow.

I was visiting a big hedge fund in New York, and one of the chief investment people told me that when the fund implements a strategy, it will buy 100 E-mini S&P futures every three seconds. And I looked at him and cutely remarked, "Well, I would sure like to have the job of pushing the button every three seconds." And he looked at me like I was from another planet, and he said, "We don't push a button."

Short-term traders can't compete against this.

Once upon a time, long, long ago, a man was being given a tour of Wall Street. He walked down to the East River, and the guide said, "Look at all these beautiful yachts out here. These are the yachts of all the big brokers." And the man responded, "Where are the customers' yachts?"

So my question today is "Where are the short-term traders' yachts?"

So I Start Researching My Own Stocks as Long-Term Holds, Right?

This question will be answered later. The short-term answer is *maybe*.

It depends on how you do it and the definition of *research* and the definition of *stocks*—and that's what I'm going to talk about next.

Fundamental research can be tricky. Information can be inaccurate.

Earnings can be pretty much what management wants them to be. Very often management will come into accounting and say, "We would like earnings to be $0.37 per share this quarter. Make earnings $0.37 per share." And they do. And they can. So you read about all sorts of things—write-offs of one-time items. These are really expenses incurred in the normal course of business, but they tend to be written off to adjust earnings.

Even Wall Street analysts are often duped when doing fundamental analysis.

Anecdote—Teaching the Analysts What They Didn't Get Taught at Harvard

Putnam, being based in Boston and being an old Boston institution, had a policy of hiring only graduates of the Harvard Business School as analysts. They were peas in a pod, all alike. I perceived that one of my jobs at Putnam was to teach the analysts the facts of investment life—the stuff they didn't learn at Harvard Business School.

One morning a stock reported earnings of $0.77 per share. An analyst came into my office, tears in his eyes, because he had been carrying an estimate of $1.20. And just the week before he had talked to the company and said, "I am estimating $1.20 for your earnings. What do you think?" And the company spokesperson had replied, "I am comfortable with that." Then the stock (which was in a downtrend, of course) responded negatively, and the analyst was upset. And the analyst asked me, "How could this happen?" And I told him, "They lied to you."

They don't teach you at the Harvard Business School that companies are going to lie to you. But I explained, "Look, they knew when you called that their earnings were going to be $0.77 per share, not $1.20. But if they had told you, they would have had to tell everybody, which they apparently were not willing to do yet. Or if they did tell you and not tell anyone else, then you would've had inside information and not be legally allowed to act on it. Or perhaps they weren't lying, but their comfort level was just substantially greater than yours. They were comfortable with your $1.20 estimate even when their actual earnings were going to be $0.77."

Is There Any Good Information in a Company's Reports?

The old saw in fundamental analysis is, "When you read an annual report, read the footnotes because that's where all the good information is buried." Companies bury it as much as they can, but if they have to include it, they put it in a footnote somewhere. So most people doing fundamental research quickly find out that it's not the numbers, it's not the report, and it's certainly not the puffery in the front of the report that are important. The real information is in the footnotes, buried in the back and in very small print.

But you can't really buy stocks using a company's report, no matter how well you understand it.

By the time you get numbers, they are already reflected in the stock price. Stock prices are a discounting mechanism. So, for instance, analysts at brokerage houses will guess that earnings will go up from $0.25 reported last quarter to $0.50 this quarter. And the stock price will rise to meet that guess. Then, if actual earnings are up but only to $0.45—a "mere" 80 percent increase—the stock price will go down. The saying goes, "Buy on the rumor; sell on the news," but small investors don't get the rumors in time and don't know how to react to the news.

Also, Wall Street just has you beat most of the time.

Richard Russell, one of the deans of Stock Market analysis, once said, "There is more human intelligence focused on the corner of Broad Street and Wall Street than any other single place on the planet." And this is true. Wall Street also has more information than you do—and gets it sooner. They've heard the rumor and acted on it.

Usually stock prices reflect news before the news even hits the airwaves.

And stocks are not the same as their companies. They are two different things. The company can do very well, and the stock not. Were I to work for somebody like Warren Buffett, who buys companies and not stocks, I would analyze companies and come up with entirely different conclusions. But I don't. All I'm ever going to "own" is a little piece of paper representing a part ownership of a company—and it's only value is the price of the shares of that stock.

And that's all most investors are ever going to own. And that's all you as an investor should care about.

And let's be clear about this up front: You *are* an investor.

And let's also assume something about you as an investor. And this assumption, which not everyone buys into, surprisingly, is that the only reason you are in the market is to *make money*. You are not in the market because you want your hunch about the Fubar Corporation to be proved right, or because you're a believer in biofuels made from house-cat dung, or because of whatever. You don't want to be known as a seer or even to write a book. You just want to make money. And if you make $10 one day by accident and $7 the next day by betting on Fubar, you know that $10 is better than $7. Period.

Technical analysis concerns itself only with that stock price— what you own. And that's where the investor has to start.

Technical analysis uses historical price data to project future data.

Isn't This Time Different? Aren't the Efficiencies in Computer Technology Creating a Whole New Paradigm?

Oh dear. The two most costly statements in investing: "This time it's different" and "It's a whole new paradigm."

"This time is different" is used to justify above-normal valuations, and these have never proved valid historically. Above-normal valuations are caused by speculative greed and often

22

turn out to be bubbles. But it's hard to see a bubble when you're in one. This time is *never* different.

And how do you know when you're in a bubble? One way is when there is such a demand for financial vehicles in a certain area that Wall Street falls all over itself creating them and bringing them to market and starts making boatloads of money from them. Wall Street is real good at doing things such as this.

And sometimes, yes, there are "whole new paradigms," but these come and go—the railroads, the "electronic boom" of the 1960s, the "nifty fifty," the Internet and e-commerce, and soon cloud computing and alternative energy. These all produced efficiencies that quickly were or will be factored into the market's calculation.

CHAPTER 2

WHAT IS TECHNICAL
ANALYSIS, AND WHY USE IT?

John Shultz of Brean Murray was a founding member of the Market Technicians Association (MTA), a professional organization I also helped found in 1972 and that I'll discuss further in Chapter 24. One of the founding documents was the "MTA Principles and Policy"; John wrote it in 1972 and was reverently referred to as the Thomas Jefferson of the MTA ever after. The "Principles and Policy" document isn't on the MTA's website, but I happen to think that it's the best thing that's ever been written explaining exactly what technical analysis is and why it is such a necessary part of the investment process. It's a wonderful starting point for us.

(And let me add a personal note: John received the MTA's Annual Award for Lifetime Achievement in 1979, the year I was president, and I was honored to be able to present it to him at our annual seminar. See Figure 2-1.)

Figure 2-1: Walter Deemer Presenting the MTA Lifetime
Achievement Award to John Shultz.

MTA Principles and Policy

The MTA asserts that the technical analysis of stock price
movements and of the supply/demand relationships underlying them can make a vital contribution to the process of
decision-making involved in efforts to preserve and enhance
the investor's capital.

The association makes this assertion on a number of
grounds, including the following considerations:

> Technical Analysis deals directly with the gener-
> ally undisputed fact that the market price of a stock
> does not necessarily—nor indeed, usually—at any
> given time coincide with its intrinsic value, which

itself is often a matter of controversy. In dealing with this frequently very elastic differential between market price and underlying value, technical analysis claims to cope with problems posed by changes in investor confidence more efficiently than conventional "fundamental" value analysis. Accordingly, technical analysis and fundamental analysis, insofar as they relate to specific common stocks and to the stock market at large, can properly be regarded as mutually complementary and, in fact, interdependent.

In a broader perspective, technical analysis concerns itself also with supply/demand relationships affecting the equity market as a whole and with potential future shifts in these relationships that may be instrumental in shaping future price movements. In pursuit of this concern, it extends to the examination of money flows, banking statistics, interest rates, etc., past, present, and potentially future. It is in this area that technical analysis borders most closely on economic and fundamental security analysis, because money flows tend to impinge on stock prices as well as on corporate earnings, and because the trend of interest rates tends to influence the market valuation of current and prospective earnings and dividends.

Moreover, the tendency of price trends to persist and of investors' behavioral patterns to recur enables the technical analyst to recognize and anticipate potentially favorable or unfavorable investment environments. Indeed, the recognition of extremes in investor psychology is one of the technical market analyst's unique contributions to the field of investment techniques.

The Association asserts, in sum, that the technical analysis of stock price movements and of the supply/demand relationships underlying them is a valid, indeed an indispensable, element in the formulation of a "reasonable basis" for investment decisions.

The Association dedicates itself to the widest possible dissemination and acceptance of these principles and to promote the highest achievable standards of professional conduct, effort, and scholarship among its members in all areas within the purview of technical analysis.

What is Technical Analaysis?

How would you define technical analysis?
First, let's define what technical analysis is not.
There are four common types of analysis.
The most common type is *fundamental analysis*. A fundamental analyst studies companies. He looks at Intel's annual report and says, "That's a well-managed company with a good cash position and 10 years of sales growth. I think I'll buy some."

Then there is *economic analysis*. An economic analyst looks at the *Wall Street Journal* and some statistics and says, "More people are expected to buy computers this year, so the market for chips will be better, so Intel's probably a good buy because it is the market leader. I think I'll buy some."

And then there is the *random walker*. That random walker knows in her heart that if Intel is a well-managed company, and if people really are going to buy computers this summer, the news is already incorporated into the price of the stock, and all stocks thus are valued appropriately. Therefore, the whole selection process is a crap shoot. So Ms Walk ignores all research of any type and says, "I think this week I'll buy every five-letter stock beginning with a vowel." And she ends up with 100 shares of Intel.

(The stock market is not, however, a random walk—no matter what the academics would have you believe. The reason was best expressed by the aforementioned John Shultz: "The stock market is not a random walk because price changes create responses on the part of investors.")

And then there is *technical analysis*. That's where you want to be.

A technical analyst focuses on only one piece of information relative to a company—the price of a share of its stock. And he buys the stock only because he believes, based on past behavior, that the price will go up. This is really the most basic part of all stock investing. Remember: A stock is not the same as the company. A stock is just a little piece of paper that represents part ownership of a company. The only reason that anyone buys one of those little pieces of paper is because they think they'll be able to sell it to someone else at a later date for a higher price.

With technical investing strategies, then, investors can cut to the chase, which is making money, and ignore the noise and hoopla. And *the chase* is as follows.

Focus on Price

A technical analyst analyzes what she actually buys and sells. She doesn't buy the company or its prospects. She buys a share of stock.

Remember that stock is of value only to the holder, not to the company. The company it represents gave birth to the stock a while ago—sometimes, a very, very long while ago—and now it is just a piece of paper that lives pretty much on its own. The company gets no benefit from the subsequent buying and selling of the stock. And that stock is not the virgin stock the company issued: It's been whoring around all over the place. It's been traded, it's been manipulated, it gets talked about, and rumors affect its value.

But its current price is its only value.

It is also the only hard number you have to work with.

Because the only true number on Wall Street is the stock price. It's the only thing that cannot be fudged. It can be manipulated, but it can't be fudged. Right now, right this minute, you know exactly what the price of your stock is. You may not agree with it, you may think that it is way out of line, but that's what it is. It's not adjusted seasonally. It's not normalized. It is the price, in American dollars, that your share of stock is worth right now. It won't be the same tomorrow morning. It wasn't the same this morning. But that's what it is.

So basically a technical analyst concerns himself with analyzing the stock price rather than anything else. Where has the price been? Where is it heading?

There are only two directions—up and down.

Concentrate on Trends

Investors try too hard to gaze into a crystal ball and figure out *why* a stock might move up or down. But they shouldn't do that. Even after the fact—after their prize stock takes a sudden 10 percent dip—they can never really know why prices rose or fell on a particular day. For every price move, there can be many external reasons and an infinite number of internal ones.

The reasons may or may not have something to do with what the company is doing. The stock price may go up (or down) because the company reports better (or worse) earnings. It may go down (or up) because some international incident takes place somewhere in the Mideast. Something happens to the price of oil. Something happens politically. Something happens economically on a macro basis. Some high-frequency trader swoops in and swoops out. Or some fund manager gets up on the wrong side of bed and just decides to sell it. Nothing has changed about the company from the day before except that one powerful person has decided to sell its stock.

So what does cause price changes?

All price changes are caused by an imbalance in supply and demand. That's it. There are more sellers than buyers, or there are more buyers than sellers. Anything that creates or changes supply and demand is of interest to a technically savvy investor.

And how can technical analysis predict price changes?

Classical technical analysis means analyzing the past trends in a stock's price to see where future prices might go. Analysts look at historic prices to detect patterns, trends, and momentum and try to project the stock price into the future.

At its most basic, remember that trends happen. Randomness indicates that on any given day, a stock price is 50 percent likely to go up and 50 percent likely to go down. But we all know that this isn't really true. Prices may go up one day and down the next, but over time, prices trend up, and they trend down. So, if a stock went up in January, it is more than 50 percent likely that it will go up in February. Ditto March. A body in motion tends to stay in motion.

Tracking movements that follow a pattern can help you to make better buy-sell decisions.

Be an Investor, Not a Trader— Think Longer Term

In the last 10 years or so, technical analysis has been applied more and more to shorter and shorter time frames. Market players look for pattern recognition, trend changes, and momentum shifts that take place on very short-term time frames—minute-by-minute ones in many cases. But investors should use technical analysis with a long-term investment horizon and resist the temptation to try to forecast very short-term moves with it.

Here I should quote Ken Safian, who with Ken Smilen developed the *dual-market principal* in the late 1950s. Ken (Safian) told me once, "It's unfortunate that the short-term orientation of most technicians has given all of us a bad name." I was so impressed by this that I wrote it down, and I still have that piece of paper years and years later to remind me that the real value of technical analysis is in analyzing long-term trends, not intraday trends.

Why should technical analysis be applied to longer time frames?

First, although it has become exponentially easier for individual investors to trade on a very short-term basis using their computers and an e-trade account, it has become exponentially harder for them to make any money doing it.

Take your broker's trading service. Who do you think that system was developed for? It was developed to turn a profit for its developers, not for you. So your trading account package is full of technical tools—numbers and charts that encourage you to actively trade; lots of trades generate lots of commission revenue for the broker. Making you anxious makes them money.

Also, Wall Street has stacked the deck against the short-term trader.

Individual investors with their e-trade accounts now compete against high-frequency trading (HFT) operations with massive computer banks that analyze data and execute programmed trades in just milliseconds. This makes charts irrelevant. By the time a human can put a chart together on a screen, the computer's high-frequency trading algorithms already have responded and bought and sold the stock.

This has resulted in the nonsense of high-frequency traders putting their servers right next to the exchange servers so that they don't lose valuable time in having the data sent all the way from New York to Boston and then back again because by then the server right next to the exchange server has already done the trade in time that is measured in milliseconds. It's gotten to the point where HFT firms that have computers right next to the exchange servers have to pay higher rents than firms with computers on the other side of the room.

But high-frequency computer trading can be very, very dangerous. If someone makes a mistake programming the computer, it can be a disaster. In the old days, if somebody sent an order in to buy $1 million worth of something, and she made a mistake and it came in as $1 billion, somebody would look at the order and say, "Oh, somebody put the comma in the wrong place. I'm going to ask whether that's okay." Computers don't do that; they just automatically execute the order, and then all sorts of mean, nasty things happen because you've taken the human oversight away. The trades take place before a human can intervene. And all of a sudden, the trading has made the 6:00 news.

Just think back to the "flash crash" of May 2010, when the Dow Jones went down 600 points in a couple of minutes and then went back up 600 points in a couple of minutes. A computer in the Midwest was told to sell so many Standard & Poor's (S&P) futures contracts every five minutes, taking no more than 30 percent of the volume during the preceding five-minute period. But the supposedly all-knowing programmers somehow forgot to tell the computer that if prices were going straight down and it was doing 30 percent of the volume that there should be some sort of price limit involved as well.

The computer wasn't just taking 30 percent of the volume on a one-shot deal; it was moving the market to the downside. And because the market moved, the computer would respond—every five minutes. And prices were cascading lower. No one ever bothered to tell the computer to check to see if prices were falling apart at the same time. The programmers forgot to put that little parameter in. There were no humans involved to say, "Hey, maybe we should check before we push the button again."

So computer trading is a problem. And the amount of short-term trading done by computer is staggering. I've been told that on any given day computer trading can represent upwards of 60 percent and sporadically up to 80 percent of the total volume.

This is something that institutional investors understand. They know to what extent it's them against the machine. But, in a sense, they are the machine. They control the algorithms. By volume, there is more trading being done by PhDs in math than there is by people with an understanding of industry and the economy.

But there's more.

Complexity

The sheer number of markets and indices has grown and gotten more complex—and everything is now interlinked—futures, options, and exchange-traded funds (ETFs, which are baskets of stocks). So, for example, if you put a buy or sell order in for one component stock in the S&P 500 Index, not only does that individual stock go up or down, but the order changes a whole raft of other things: the S&P 500 Index, the S&P 500 Index futures contract, options on the S&P 500 Index, ETFs involving the S&P 500 Index, a whole bunch of sector ETFs, and a whole matrix of other things. Linda Raschke, at an American Association of Professional Technical Analysts conference, put it like this:

"Everybody is sitting around watching, and all of a sudden somebody comes in with an order, and everybody else just dogpiles on."

That one order, in just one stock, creates ripple effects through the whole market. Let's say that the stock goes up. This changes the S&P 500, and it also changes the S&P 500 relative to the Russell 2000 Index. The stock, if it happens to be Intel, changes the semiconductor ETF. The semiconductor ETF is now changed relative to the technology ETF. Algorithms kick in all over the place.

And that's just if you, an individual investor, buy the stock.

Now think of what happens when an institution buys 100,000 shares of Intel. Suddenly all the computers go haywire, and they adjust everything relative to everything else, and zillions and zillions of shares and contracts trade just because of that one order. In seconds! Blink and it's over.

And where does that leave the small investor? It leaves him with confusing short-term market signals at the very least. At the most, it leaves him without room and time to move.

These are all reasons you shouldn't focus on the short term.

So that's why I can't invest short term. Why should I invest long term?

Most of us invest over much of our adult lives, and we save primarily for retirement. We have 30, 40, or 50 years of part-time investing work ahead of us. An investment account is a long-term asset and should be treated as such.

How would you feel if you followed the value of your house on a day-to-day basis? "News flash! Hurricane forms off the Cape Verde islands in the far eastern Atlantic and may pose a threat to Florida in the next two weeks." Bang! Florida real estate goes down 82 points. "News flash: Hurricane dissipates." Bang! Florida real estate market goes back up.

So don't look at the short-term moves, minute by minute, day by day. Look at the big picture.

Ignore Noise

Investors should ignore day-to-day external distractions, particularly the news.

It gives investors a warm, fuzzy feeling to watch the news and think that it affects them personally. "The news says nuclear power is more dangerous than we think. I'm going to short nuclear and buy solar."

Small investors often make buy or sell decisions based on the news, but by then it's usually too late. Market action leads the news. The market is a leading indicator. It leads the news, and it leads economic trends.

Always remember that there is more human intelligence focused on Wall Street than any other place on earth. All these people are trying to figure out what the value of stocks should be. They have some of the world's best degrees from the most prestigious universities. They use the best computers. They have limitless research departments. And they use all sorts of different approaches. They use fundamental analysis, technical analysis, the news, rumors, even astrology—anything that seems to work.

So there is all sorts of brainpower focused on the stock market.

And collectively, all that intelligence says, "I think bad things may happen." And then the bad things happen. Well, the stock market is a discounting mechanism. It foresaw what was happening. It told you what was going to happen before it happened.

The financial news purports to explain why a stock has gone up or down, but the news media always explain it in terms of cause and effect. They say, "The market went down yesterday *because* investors were nervous about growing tensions in the Middle East." Or "The market went up yesterday *despite* investor nervousness with growing tensions in the Middle East." It's the same story in both cases; you write it both ways, you wait until the end of the day, and then you select the one that fits. It has nothing to do with reality. Your audience "needs" to know a reason why, and you have supplied them with one.

Are there times when the news affects the market? Sure. Totally unexpected and unpredictable developments always will have an impact on the market. More often, though, the news will affect the market after a long bull or bear market, when stocks are already undervalued and additional bad news comes out, and investors panic near the bottom, or when stocks are already overvalued, and small investors hear glowing news reports, climb aboard, and create a bubble.

This is not where you want to be.

One of my classic recommendations is to watch CNBC like the pros do—turn the sound off! Back in the 1980s, I had two televisions sitting one on top of each other in my office. One was tuned to CNBC—with the sound off—and the other was on CNN. In 1990, during the Gulf War, all the trading rooms put in a monitor for CNN next to their CNBC monitor. Now every trading room in the world has them, but if you look closely, you'll see that there's not a single CNBC monitor in a trading room that has the sound on.

Ordinarily, then, the news doesn't matter. Here's a good example.

Anecdote—The Kennedy Assassination

My most memorable day on Wall Street was one of my first.

I began my Wall Street career in the summer of 1963 as a research trainee at Merrill Lynch. By November, I was working on the wire inquiry desk, which responded to research-related inquiries from the branches.

Merrill's tape-monitoring unit was right around the corner from us, and since there were no quote machines in those days, it was the only place we could go to check the market. There were six desks arranged in a rectangle. The old stock ticker that ground out 500 characters per minute was to the right of the first desk, and the Merrill Lynch newswire—a great big clunky floor-model Teletype machine—was directly below it. The stock tape ran around all six desks at eye level. Bill Hinson, the senior tape watcher, had the first desk, and Jim Schuster, his assistant, had the middle desk. Forrest Frey was at the far end, with the Dow Jones news ticker at his left elbow. None of them could see the Merrill Lynch newswire without either getting up or seriously craning their neck, so if someone was hovering at the ticker checking the market, he read the headlines aloud.

Early in the afternoon of November 22, I was taking a break and checking the market. I was leaning on the newswire watching the tape when the Teletype haltingly printed out, letter by letter, the word "F-L-A-S-H," and the bell rang four times.

The newswire then transmitted, letter by letter, the words that would stun the world:

"UPI REPORTS KENNEDY SERIOUSLY WOUNDED, PERHAPS FATALLY BY ASSASSIN WHO SHOT AT HIS MOTORCADE IN DALLAS."

(I managed to Xerox a copy of the newswire with that story. You can see it—exactly as it was transmitted that fateful afternoon—in Figure 2-2.)

The Dow Jones ticker hadn't printed this yet, so we were all now just standing around with our mouths open in stunned silence. We learned afterward that our Merrill Lynch newsroom, down on the second floor of our building, was retransmitting what had come over the UPI newswire, and UPI had scooped the story.

When the shooting occurred, Merriman Smith of UPI was in the front seat of the press car that was following the presidential limousine. Smith happened to be sitting next to the one and only radio phone. So, when it happened, he grabbed the radio phone and dictated a flash to the UPI office. And the Associated Press reporter, sitting in the backseat, twitched mightily but was unable to contact his office. So UPI had the first bulletin, nobody else.

Bill Karp, who was in charge of the Merrill Lynch newswire, had read the UPI account but held back to wait for a

Figure 2-2: Photocopy of Breaking News Report of Assassination Attempt on President John F. Kennedy.

```
                                              67      2.80

      50M                    2 7/8 PC          4/1/65   2.40
      55M                      "              66       2.65

$665,000 UNIVERSITY OF MINNESOTA DORMITORY BONDS  NOT RATED
      50M                    2 1/8 PC          10/1/65  2.35
        "                      "                66      2.50
        "          '           "                67      2.65
        "                      "                68      2.80

      35M                    2 3/4 PC          9/1/64   2.10
      90M                      "                65      2.35
        "                      "                66      2.50
      S5M                      "                67      2.65

$120,000 RUTGERS UNIVERSITY HOUSING AND DINING BONDS S AND P A
      40M                    2 3/4 PC          5/1/65   2.30
        "                      "                66      2.55

CONCESSIONS - 1/8 64-65
              1/4 BALANCE

ORDERS -    TO BREZ - KN
                      KN 133P



      DJ 130 PM AVERAGES
INDL 735.96  UP 3.31 OR 0.45 PC
RAIL 170.28  UP 0.59 OR 0.35 PC
UTIL 136.63 OFF 0.29 OR 0.21 PC
STKS 258.98  UP 0.77 OR 0.30 PC
                              135P



DJ - REG MISSISSIPPI RIVER FUEL 45C DIV 12/30 12/13
                                        136P




      FLASH 0000


   UPI REPORTS KENNEDY SERIOUSLY WOUNDED . PERHAPS FATALLY BY
ASSASSIN WHO SHOT AT HIS MOTORCADE IN DALLAS .
                                  139P 00000

00000000
```

41

confirmation. A minute or two later, bells started going off elsewhere in the newsroom, and he immediately dictated the flash. So we were three minutes ahead of Dow Jones on that one.

The stock market did what it does best in response to sudden, shocking events: It started going down. And the specialists on the New York Stock Exchange did what they did best when that happens: They went to hide. Some of them actually sold short into the decline, which they are absolutely not supposed to do, and they got into a bit of trouble because of that. And the market kept going down. The first bulletin came across the Merrill Lynch newswire at 1:39 p.m. The first bulletin came across Dow Jones at 1:42 p.m. And the managers shut down the exchange at 2:07 p.m. because investors were panicking and prices were tumbling. (The Dow Jones Industrials, which had been 735 at 1:30, had plunged to 711 when trading was abruptly halted.)

In the face of possible investor panic, Merrill Lynch decided to keep its branch offices open Saturday with a skeleton staff and asked for volunteers to come in and man the wire-inquiry desk. I lived two subway stops away, so I volunteered.

I arrived Saturday to an eerily quiet building. There were three or four of us sitting around, doing nothing. Not a single wire came in that day about the assassination and its possible repercussions. The only question that came in that day, in fact, was about Ling-Temco-Vought (LTV), one of the very early conglomerates. It was in the midst of a very involved process spinning off three subsidiaries: a sporting goods company, a pharmaceutical company, and a meatpacking company (which Wall Street had dubbed "Golf Ball, Goofball, and Meatball"), and one of the branches asked about the mechanics of the spinoffs.

The Dow Jones Industrials went from 735 to 711 on Friday when the exchange was closed. When it reopened on Tuesday, though, the Dow retraced the ground it had lost and then some, as if nothing had happened, closing at 743. Investors realized that America was going to go on. Even though, some horrible act had taken place, America still was going to go on.

CHAPTER 3

HOW HARD IS IT? CAN I DO IT?

Bob Farrell's 10 Rules

Bob Farrell, who worked at Merrill Lynch throughout his career, is unquestionably the most highly respected technical analyst of them all. Just how highly respected? At a long-ago Contrary Opinion Forum in Vermont, the Friday evening session had to be delayed because Bob was the special guest on *Wall Street Week*, and we had all gathered around the television to watch him rather than going to the meeting location.

I had the privilege of working for Bob at Merrill Lynch when I was fresh out of college, impressionable, and eager to learn. His teachings were always succinct, logical, and delivered in plain English. I have been fortunate to have had him as a mentor throughout my Wall Street career and have always tried to follow his teachings both in substance and in style.

Bob published his list of "Ten Market Rules to Remember" in 2001. These contain the basic precepts behind technical analysis—and contain more wisdom than any 10 things that haven't been written on two tablets of stone.

There are varying versions of the 10 rules on the Internet, so I asked Bob what his "official" version was. Here's what he sent me—together with a new, eleventh rule. I am reprinting them with his permission.

1. Markets tend to return to the mean over time.
2. Excesses in one direction will lead to an opposite excess in the other direction.
3. There are no new eras—excesses are never permanent.
4. Exponentially rapidly rising or falling markets usually go further than you think, but they do not correct by going sideways.
5. The public buys the most at a top and the least at a bottom.
6. Fear and greed are stronger than long-term resolve.
7. [Bull] . . . markets are strongest when they are broad and when they narrow to a handful of blue chip names.
8. Bear markets have three stages—sharp down, reflexive rebound, [and] a drawn-out fundamental downtrend.
9. When the experts and forecasts agree—something else is going to happen.
10. Bull markets are more fun than bear markets.

And here is Bob's new rule:

11. Though business conditions may change, corporations and securities may change, and financial institutions

and regulations may change, human nature remains essentially the same.

I wouldn't presume to annotate a single one of those rules; each one easily stands on its own merits, and they are reprinted here just as the Master originally wrote them. I do want to take a minute, though, to explain just why I think they are so important.

Technical analysis, you see, is much, much more than mechanically interpreting a chart or some data. It is much, much more than simply looking at even the very best charts that are available and the very best indicators that you can find. And what Bob Farrell's rules do is to elevate you past the basics; they make you think about the stock market and your investments, not just follow them via some mechanical interpretations of some rules.

Bob Farrell's Rules, in other words, are designed to make you look at the market intellectually, not mechanically. And elevating yourself to that higher plane will help make you a technically savvy investor.

PART II

PRINCIPLES AND USES OF TECHNICAL ANALYSIS

CHAPTER 4

PRINCIPLES—SUPPLY/DEMAND AND SENTIMENT

The two basic principles of technical analysis are supply/ demand and sentiment. Since these principles have specific definitions and parameters as applied to technical analysis, a brief discussion of each follows.

Supply/Demand

Investors have only one absolute number with which to work— price; that price is set every time there is a transaction between a willing buyer and a willing seller.

The numbers of sellers and buyers are never in equilibrium. Sometimes there are more buyers than sellers, and the price of the stock goes up. Rising prices create an optimistic or bull market in the stock. When there are more sellers than buyers, the price goes down. Falling prices create a pessimistic or bear market.

Technical analysts don't ask why a stock is bought or sold. We simply don't care. All we want to know is what. What happened? The price changed. It went up, or it went down. There are more buyers out there or more sellers. More demand or more supply.

Supply and demand can be seen in a number of ways. Change in price is the most concrete.

But there are other measures of supply and demand. Total volume of sales, volatility of prices, and the futures and options markets all can measure aspects of supply and demand. But in the end, it all boils down to just one simple thing—price.

Sentiment

Market sentiment is an important concept, but many people don't understand the term as it relates to investing. They sometimes assume that technical analysts measure the "sentiment" with which investors make buying decisions. This point of view, though, puts the cart before the horse because we can't know what individual investors feel.

Each individual decision to buy or sell is different. The decisions can be rational or irrational, market-based or non-market-based. Somebody watched the football game today, and his team lost, and he is so discouraged that he is going to go in and dump something tomorrow. If his team had won, he might act differently. So the fact that one team lost today and ticked somebody off affected the price of the stock.

Somebody can say, "Jupiter and Saturn are in opposition, so I am selling drug stocks." You may think that this is the most ridiculous thing you've ever heard in your life. But, if someone comes in and sells drug stocks because of it, she is affecting the market. So even astrology affects the market—not in a causal way, but in a derived way, because it caused somebody to do something, and that made the price of a security go up or down.

The same human sentiment may even provoke different reactions. For instance, if Overtraded.com released earnings that were better than expectations, investors with the same sentiment ("Well, the earnings are better than I'd hoped") may take different actions. One may buy ("That's good news!"), whereas another may sell ("The good news is out; what will they do for an encore?"). Both have good reasons for their decisions, but only one will emerge ultimately triumphant in the marketplace—and the price action will tell you who.

Market sentiment reflects what investors think and feel, but as measured by how they respond, which is to sell or buy stocks with the expectation of making a profit. By selling and buying, they move the price up and down and change the numbers of buyers relative to the number of sellers. More buyers → prices up → market optimistic; more sellers → prices down → market pessimistic. Market actions—and the human emotions in response to them—create sentiment indicators. And you don't really care *why* the sentiment is there, just that it is and that it can be measured.

There are a number of paired adjectives to describe market sentiment: *optimism* (or *enthusiasm*) and *pessimism*, *exuberance* (or *euphoria*) and *despair*. At the extreme, optimism is sometimes called *irrational exuberance* or *mania*. They differ, if they differ at all, only in degree. One side means that investors are positive; the other side means that investors are negative.

During periods of optimism, sentiment measures greed—how much investors think they can make in the future. During periods of pessimism, it measures risk—how much investors think they could lose in the future.

This is very much like the market's reaction to news. The market reacts to what it thinks will happen in the future and not what's happening now. If investors think that prices will continue to rise, they will act on that assumption. Conversely, if they think that prices will continue to fall, they will act on that assumption.

All stocks, all market sectors, and even the broad market go through periods of optimism and pessimism. They trend upward, or they trend downward. This creates buying and selling opportunities for technically savvy investors.

(Just how important is sentiment? It's been said that a good psychologist can make more money in the stock market than a good economist!)

Is Optimism to Pessimism the Same Concept as Overvalued to Undervalued?

No. *Overvalued* and *undervalued* are concepts used by fundamental analysts and refer to the condition of a company relative to its stock price. *Optimism* and *pessimism* are technical terms that refer to how investors think of the stock price. In addition, *overvalued* is a statistical concept ("The price is too high relative to earnings"), and *optimism* is a psychological concept ("The price is high—but it's going even higher").

Where Is the Most Extreme Sentiment in a Market?

Fear is a much stronger emotion than greed, so bear markets are more emotional than bull markets. And bear markets are especially emotional because the news—and the emotions among investors that are triggered in response to the news—is so negative. The most extreme sentiment is found at a bear market bottom.

How About the Top, during Periods of Irrational Exuberance? The Tech Bubble, for Instance?

There are periods in bull markets when prices seem to have gone up higher than they should, for longer than they should, or faster than they should. At the extreme, they can create a bubble, which ultimately will burst with unpleasant consequences. The tech wreck that began in 2000 was an instance of that. Big professional investors got out fairly early on, but smaller investors drove the market up beyond most expectations. The latecomers thought that prices were going to increase like that forever.

This is an example of the irrational belief discussed earlier, to wit: "It's a whole new paradigm. This time it's different."

The four most costly words in investing, in fact, are *This time is different*. This time it's going to keep going up indefinitely. This time the laws don't work. But that's true only until it doesn't keep going up. Until the laws do work again—as they always do ultimately.

What About Irrational Negativity? Are There Negative Versions of Bubbles?

Yes. Declining markets create nervousness, then concern, then fear, then—after they've gone down a whole lot—panic, as investors project the now-severe price declines into the future (which is all too easy to do with the negative headlines that always appear after a big decline) and sell on the inevitable and irrational downside fear. This time it's different. This time it's Armageddon, and prices are going to keep falling forever.

But they won't. The stocks are still worth something; the companies are still there, and they are still functioning. And nothing has changed since a week ago except that prices have gone down.

On both the upside and the downside, investors can tell themselves that this time behavior is going to change. This time it's going to be different.

But it never is. Ever!

Both irrationally high and irrationally low valuations occur periodically; they're just a normal part of the long-term market cycle. Irrationality is not always present at every peak and trough, but a technical analyst expects it and prepares for it. The old saying is, "The bigger the base, the higher in space" or "The bigger the top, the steeper the drop." Big swings in one direction beget big swings in the other direction.

Unfortunately, the only way you can really learn about sentiment is to live through a couple of cycles—to live through the euphoria of the top and the despair at the bottom. Words can't really describe, for example, what things were really like at the bottom in late 2008 and early 2009. They just can't.

Here's an example:

In early October 2008, on a Thursday afternoon, I was sitting in the audience at the Contrary Opinion Forum in Vermont. The speaker assured us that the Standard & Poor's 500 Index (S&P 500), which had dropped to 985 the day before, would meet support at 960. And surely, if that failed, it would bottom out at 940. Then somebody in the back of the room waved his iPhone and yelled, "It just closed at 910."

The next day, Friday, the Dow Jones opened down 700 points. I was sitting in the audience watching it on a computer. You simply can't learn from a book just how unbelievably gut-wrenching it is when the market has gone down more than 7 percent one day and then opens down another 7 percent the next morning. You simply can't describe the feelings adequately. It's a very, very tough thing to live through. Very emotional.

How Does Technical Analysis Deal with Irrationality in the Markets?

It's hardest to deal with bottoms, with the latter stages of bear markets. To the average investor, there seems to be no rationality anywhere. The market lurches down, ignoring good news and bad, ignoring changes in the economy.

But long-term technical analysis deals with bottoms in two ways. First, it's important to think with more than a day's horizon at market bottoms. Day-to-day changes are likely to be extreme and irrational. Second, we use contrarian thinking, which assumes that if everyone is very, very bearish, they are going to be wrong sooner rather than later. Investors may be better off to wait or to trade against the prevailing trend.

During the late stages of bear markets, all the fundamental and economic indicators seem to be broken. The psychology—the sentiment—is trumping everything. Greed has been forgotten. Fear is running rampant.

But this is what the environment is like when it's the time to buy. As I've said many, many times over the years, "When the time comes to buy, you won't want to."

Anecdote—Fable of the Fishing Boat

During the 1970s, I ran Putnam's Market Analysis Department. Putnam's fund managers, though, were fundamentally oriented investors who thought that their job was to buy the best stocks on a fundamental basis and not worry about market conditions.

During the latter stages of a bear market, though, even the very best stocks fall day after day after day. During one of those bear markets, the fund managers got tired of hearing me say that the prices of even their most beloved stocks were going to keep going down, and I just wasn't able to make them understand that bear markets trump even the best fundamentals.

So I ended up writing "The Fable of the Fishing Boat," which I happen to think is the best thing I've ever written.

It's reproduced here exactly as I published it at Putnam in 1978.

I N T E R O F F I C E   M E M O R A N D U M

TO: Investment Division

FROM: Walter R. Deemer   DATE: January 12, 1978

THE FABLE OF THE FISHING BOAT

Once upon a time there was a big fishing boat in the North Atlantic. One day the crew members noticed that the barometer had fallen sharply, but since it was a warm, sunny and peaceful day they decided to pay it no attention and went on with their fishing.

The next day dawned stormy, and the barometer had fallen further, so the crew decided to have a meeting and discuss what to do.

"I think we should keep in mind that we are fishermen," said the first to speak. "Our job is to catch as many fish as we can; this is what everyone ashore expects of us. Let us concentrate on this and leave the worrying about storms to the weathermen."

"Not only that," said the next, "but I understand that the weathermen are all predicting a storm. Using contrary opinion, we should expect a sunny day and, therefore, should not worry about the weather."

"Yes," said a third crew member, "and keep in mind that since this storm got so bad so quickly that it is likely to expend itself soon. It has already become overblown."

The crew thus decided to continue with their business as usual.

The next morning saw frightful wind and rain following steadily deteriorating conditions all the previous day. The barometer continued to fall. The crew held another meeting.

"Things are about as bad as they can get," said one. "The only time they were worse was in 1974, and we all know that was due to the unusual pressure systems that were centered over the Middle East that won't be repeated. We should, therefore, expect things to get better."

59

- 2 -

So the crew continued to cast their nets as usual. But a strange thing happened: the storm was carrying unusually large and fine fish into their nets, yet at the same time the violence was ripping the nets loose and washing them away. And the barometer continued to fall.

The crew gathered together once more.

"This storm is distracting us way too much from our regular tasks," complained one person, struggling to keep his feet. "We are letting too many fish get away."

"Yes," agreed another as everything slid off the table, "and furthermore, we are wasting entirely too much time in meetings lately. We are missing too much valuable fishing time."

"There's only one thing to do," said a crew member. "That's right!" "Aye!" they all shouted.

So they threw the barometer overboard.

(Editors Note: The above manuscript, now preserved in a museum, was originally discovered washed up on a desolate island above the north coast of Norway, about halfway to Spitsbergen.)

WRD

/ls

60

It's that subtle reference to a desolate island in the last paragraph that elevated this to the best thing I ever wrote. Putnam's weekly Investment Division meeting, you see, was held in the Trustees Room, and a huge black-and-white world map covered one whole wall. It is doubtful that any of the money managers ever looked at the map, but if they had, they would have seen there is indeed a desolate island off the north coast of Norway, about halfway to Spitsbergen.

It's called Bear Island.

CHAPTER 5

USES—TIMING AND SELECTION

The basic uses of technical analysis are for timing (when to buy or sell) and stock/sector selection (what to buy or sell).

Market Timing

Will Rogers said it first:

"The way to make money in the stock market is this: You buy some good stock and hold it until it goes up; then sell it. If it don't go up, don't buy it."

Technical analysts believe that there is a time to buy and a time to sell even the best stocks.

No stock goes up forever. Its price goes up and down in cycles. Markets repeat themselves according to a logical progression that can be measured over time. They trend up and trend down. They cycle through periods of optimism, followed by periods of pessimism.

Bob Farrell said it best: "History never repeats itself exactly, but human behavior does."

All market actions should be evaluated in terms of timing. What is the cycle? Where in the cycle are you?

My Broker Says He Never Times the Market

Some of the conventional wisdom tells us that market timing is not a good thing because it's too risky. However, if you think about it a little, all brokers do some market timing. They just don't call it that.

Every time your broker sees a stock that he says is "undervalued," he's making a judgment that it's a good thing to buy it now. Ditto an "overvalued" stock that he recommends selling.

My Broker Says Market Timing Is Wrong Because the Market Gains Most During Strong Upside Days, and I Might Miss Them

All too often something crosses my desk that tries to debunk market timing by showing how much upside appreciation long-term investors would lose if they were out of the market on its 10 or 20 best days, weeks, or some such.

The lost upside appreciation they've calculated is, admittedly, a big number. The problem is that they never get around to mentioning how much investors would avoid *losing* if they were out of the market on its worst days or weeks—and factoring in that all-important other side of the story makes all the difference in the world.

Consider the following statistics compiled by independent analyst Gary Fritz:

From January 1, 1990, until May 20, 2011—just over 1100 weeks—the Standard & Poor's 500 Index (S&P 500) gained 278 percent.

If you were not in the market during its 20 best weeks, rather than being up 278 percent, you'd be down 1.3 percent—the typically horrible figure these studies tend to produce.

But, Gary went on, if you were not in the market during the 20 worst weeks, you'd be up an incredible 1,737 percent.

And this is the really astounding bottom-line number that I'd never seen before: If you were out of the market during both its 20 best weeks and its 20 worst weeks, you'd still be up 380 percent.

This means that if you were successful in avoiding the 20 worst weeks in the stock market since 1990—but only at the cost of missing the 20 best weeks—you'd still come out way ahead of the game—380 to 278 percent!

When I reported this initially, I was asked why we should bother with exercises such as these because identifying the 20 best and 20 worst weeks is hardly a given, especially since the best- and worst-week periods tend to occur together at bottoms (although a few of the market's 20 best weeks did occur just before an important top). This means that if you were out of the market during the 20 worst weeks—as it headed into the bottoms—you also were pretty likely to be out of the market during its 20 best weeks—the rebounds from those bottoms. The key finding of Fritz's study, then, was that even if the price you paid for being out of the market during its sickening plunges into the bottom also was being out of it during those strong rebounds from the bottom, you'd still be ahead of the game—380 to 278 percent!

And that's why I said—and I still say: *Market timing works!*

And you don't have to buy at the very bottom and sell at the very top to be successful doing it.

Let me add a quote by Bernard Baruch:

"Don't try to buy at the bottom and sell at the top. That can't be done, except by liars."

Mechanics of Market Timing

Market cycles generally can be divided into four phases:

1. Everything goes up, including the averages.
2. Most stocks go up, and the averages keep going up.
3. Some stocks go up, but the averages turn down.
4. Nothing goes up, including the averages.

How Do You Know When to Buy and When to Sell?

Many of the cues are visual (Figure 5-1), and we'll discuss them in detail in the section on charts. But generally, going with the dominant trend is the way to go. Buy during an up market; sell during a down market. There's an old Wall Street saying, "Don't fight the tape." If the market is trending in one direction, never assume that it will reverse just because you think prices should be different. Prices are what they are. Are they trending up or down? If they start trending up, now's the time to buy. If they start trending down, now's the time to sell. You can always buy it back later. It's just a piece of paper. You're not married to it.

Figure 5-1: Simple Four-Year Cycle Chart.

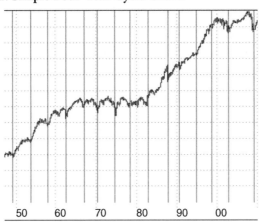

How Do You Know When It's Time to Buy?

This is hard.

Once upon a time at Putnam, I said, "I think the market is going to go down." And the market did indeed start to go down. The fund managers came into my office and said, "Aha, the stock market is starting to go down. Is it time to buy?" And I said, "Not yet." Then we had our weekly meeting. And the fund managers asked, "Is it time to buy? The stock market has gone down some more." And I said, "Not yet." And the stock market went down even further, and the fund managers came into my office and said, "Is it time to buy now?" And I said, "No, not yet." And finally, after I got tired of telling them "Not yet" all the time, I uttered what has now become a legendary phrase: "When the time comes to buy, you won't want to."

A bull market starts after a bottoming period. So there has been pessimism, and everyone who wants to sell pretty much has done so. One thing to look for is when the market stops going down on bad news—and then, in advance of the news, starts to rise.

Remember, the market leads the news.

The 10 best days in a bull market are usually right near the beginning of a cycle. That's when the professional traders and institutional money come in and before the media have a chance to analyze just why the market is going up. Then, after a while, everyone else reads the news and piles on. And as long as there are more buyers than sellers, the market will continue to rise. And finally, everyone who wants to buy has bought, and prices stop going up.

How Do You Know When the Market Has Topped? How Do You Know When to Sell?

First and foremost, gauge market sentiment. When the time comes to sell, you won't want to.

At some point everyone who wants to buy has bought, and prices will stop going up. That is a bull market top.

At a bull market top, the market advance usually slows over a lengthy period of time. No one wants to sell. Everyone is happy. Everyone thinks that the market will keep going higher. The newspapers are full of glowing headlines and reports. It takes a bit of intestinal fortitude to say that this news is the reason why the market has already gone up, and it therefore may be time to back away and do some selling.

When everyone who wants to buy has bought, there is usually not much for sale. But unlike, say, commodities, where fear of scarcity causes price spikes, prices tend to remain steadier than seems normal.

Market tops usually take a while to form. There is usually time to get out. But always remember: When the time comes to sell, you won't want to; the news is always good—very good— at a top.

But if you miss getting out at the very top, which most of us do, one way to keep small losses from becoming big ones is to sell stocks you own if they fall below a long-term moving average; say, of 30 weeks. Remember — you can always buy it back.

There Is "Usually" Time to Get Out. Is This Always True?

Not always. Speculative bubbles may lead to dramatic peaks and crashes.

In 1929, the market crashed. It was the beginning of a decline that took the Dow Jones from 380 in 1929 to 40 in 1932 and there was hardly any top on the charts at all. The top was barely visible on the monthly chart and wasn't all that big on the weekly chart. The market basically ran up, reversed, and then ran back down again.

We saw this also with the Nasdaq peak in 2000 (Figure 5-2).

Almost everyone saw that the Nasdaq dot-com run-up had become a huge speculative mania. Sophisticated investors pretty much backed away from it prematurely, before the top. But the psychology had built up so much that enough money came in from the public to keep the merry-go-round spinning, keep the game going, and it managed to keep things going

Figure 5-2: Nasdaq Peak in 2000.

Chart courtesy of DecisionPoint.com

well in excess of its natural end. But when the Nasdaq finally reversed, it did so very, very quickly.

And it's not just stocks. When gold topped at $850 in 1980, the reversal and top were just one day in length.

Manias/fads/bubbles always go up longer than rational people think they can. As John Maynard Keynes once famously remarked, "Markets can remain irrational longer than you can remain solvent." Manias/fads/bubbles, though, all end very badly. To quote Bob Farrell, "Exponential rapidly rising . . . markets usually go further than you think, but they do not correct by going sideways." Bubbles thus are ultrarisky events both during their final stages on the way up and when they finally reverse.

When Is a Good Time to Sell?

As I said, market tops usually end gradually. Then prices start falling, slowly.

As prices start to fall, you're in a bear market.

Institutional investors usually try to get out near the beginning of a decline, that is, at the end of a market top. As they start to get out, prices start to fall. Then the news tries to explain the falling prices, and then selling intensity starts building.

Usually, a bear market does not start with a horrific decline; the horrific declines usually occur more than halfway down, when investors get spooked. They look for news developments that might be causing the declines and then react to the news by selling.

Market bottoms are a lot more volatile than market tops because fear is a much stronger, much more powerful emotion than greed.

The market, as it goes through a bottoming process, will make sickening lurches to the downside. Very often those days are the worst days in market history. The reasons for the market rout are obvious. The media are full of bleak headlines and reasons why the market has gone down. It is a very emotional time.

Everyone is involved in the selling process.

Near the top of a bull market, most buying is done by unsophisticated investors who are anxious not to be left behind. At the bottom, though, there is a wide range of selling. Individual investors—both sophisticated and unsophisticated—sell, fearing still lower prices. But there is also a lot of institutional selling at the bottom. Sometimes institutions have to sell to meet redemption requests. Often, though, it involves forced selling by institutions and people who have bought stocks on credit (*margin calls*). I'll discuss this in Chapter 11.

So When Is a Bear Market Over?

Look for evidence that the market has stopped going down on bad news. All the reasons that the market has gone down will be painfully obvious at a bear market bottom. The news background will be extremely pessimistic. Remember, though, that the market is a discounting mechanism, so if it has gone down 20 percent, the reasons why it went down will be obvious—after it has already gone down. So look for the first tentative signs that the market is starting to shrug off bad news. When it does, it tells you that the market may have discounted the worst and may be starting to anticipate the better things that inevitably will follow. The market's discounting function is always—always—looking ahead, and when the market starts to shrug off bad news, it may be beginning to sense reasons why the next move may be up rather than down.

Individual investors, too, can afford the luxury of waiting for the market to start going up before they buy. Remember two things: First, the biggest price drops are right before the biggest price gains. Second, the gains are likely to be sudden.

Humans/investors always have a psychological tendency to project the past into the future. Therefore, if prices have been going down, and the fundamental background is negative, which it has to be for prices to have gone down, the natural tendency is for investors to project those prices into the future.

But the market always—always—looks into the future, not at the present. It is always looking around the next bend. So by the time we are aware of why the market has done something, it has usually finished doing it.

In fact, the news speaks to both bull and bear markets—but in a counterintuitive way. Here's a definition from Harold Ehrlich, who was with Shearson at the time and later became president and then chairman of Bernstein-Macaulay: "A bull market is when stocks don't go down on bad news. A bear market is when stocks don't go up on good news."

This is why most people are bullish at a high (when they should sell) and bearish at a low (when they should buy).

Are Tops and Bottoms Created Equal?

No. Fear is a *much* stronger emotion than greed. Humans are programmed that way, I'm told, because it ensures their survival. (Check the locks before you go to bed! Practice fire drills!)

Long-cycle bottoms can be particularly hard to fathom.

One famous story is that in the year 1938, when the stock market was still recovering from the crash of 1929 and had lurched along for years and years and years, essentially doing nothing, only three members of the graduating class of Harvard Business School went to work on Wall Street.

To bring this into a contemporary context, my friend Dean LeBaron has said publicly, referring to the more than 100,000 members of the Financial Analysts Federation: "That's too many analysts; by the time this is over, there will only be 50,000." History thus suggests that by the time this structural bear market is all over, it may not be socially acceptable to be seeking a career on Wall Street.

What to Buy

When the market is in an uptrend, buy the market. When a sector is in an uptrend, buy the sector. When an individual stock is in an uptrend . . . well, that's a harder call.

Technically savvy investors like to spot the individual stocks that lead the market or that lead a sector, but this can be a high-risk proposition. Technical investing works best with a diversified portfolio. The legendary Peter Lynch of Fidelity's Magellan Fund said it best: "If I find 10 stocks I like, I don't know which one is going to do the best, so I buy all 10."

Also, the way the market is these days, any little piece of news can have an immense impact on the stock price on a very short-term basis. A biotech company can get a negative result from a test, and all of a sudden, its stock is down 20 percent. But if you have a package of biotech stocks, it's not going to happen to all of them at once. There's no way, though, to forecast rogue waves with individual stocks.

The thing is, in the old days, the stock would go down, but it would go down tick by tick, bump by bump. Now the stock can open 20 percent lower in the morning. When I came into this business, we never had air pockets where a stock suddenly drops 20 percent. They used to go down half a percent for 40 days to create a 20 percent decline. Now they go down 20 percent in half a second, thanks to high-frequency computers that help to generate instantaneous reactions to news events.

There is always some potentially adverse development lurking in the closet in any company, no matter how carefully you research it. A key person can die suddenly. A key competitor can become more aggressive. There can be a favorable or unfavorable development in either the company or a competitor. The environmental regulatory background can change positively or negatively. Nobody can predict these, and stock prices now are so dependent on actions by Washington and state governments, the health of key personnel, and short-term developments within the company and with its competitors that having all your eggs in one basket can be pretty tough. You need to be pretty lucky to get away with performing well with just one or two stocks.

Having said that, I need to add that you can diversify into multiple stocks through exchange-traded funds (ETFs). So, if you have an idea, for example, that biotechnology stocks are an attractive place to be, rather than going out and doing research on individual companies to find 10 biotech stocks that you think are attractive, you can buy a biotechnology ETF and have broad exposure to biotechs through that ETF. You also can invest in Fidelity's favored biotech stocks, which are constantly monitored and updated, by investing in its Select Biotechnology Fund (or, similarly, in one of their other sector funds that invests in another industry) and other firms, such as Rydex, also have biotech sector funds. [The Securities and Exchange Commission (SEC) requires a disclaimer on how you can lose money in a sector fund.] So you don't necessarily have to have a lot of names in your portfolio. You can get a lot of diversification through ETFs or mutual funds.

Anecdote—General Motors Dividend

Back in the old days, the stock of the General Motors Corporation used to be one of the bluest of blue chip stocks, but it was exceedingly cyclical. At one point when I was working at Putnam the stock had gone down from the 70s to the high 30s, but it looked like both the stock and the stock market were bottoming after a correction.

Then General Motors cut its dividend. One of the fund managers came in to our morning meeting and announced that he wanted to sell the stock. I was not in favor because it looked like the price had already bottomed. I held up the chart of the stock, which showed that the price had sunk from the 70s into the 30s, and I said, in what some people think was the greatest line ever at a Putnam morning meeting, "I'm glad the stock didn't go down in vain." What I meant, of course, was that the stock price had gone down for a reason. Investors foresaw bad things happening, and now the bad thing had happened. But since the price had already gone down in anticipation of the bad news, it didn't have to go down again now that the news was out.

Contrary Opinion

Contrary thinking just helps manage the changes in market sentiment. Its basic premise is that if sentiment is lopsided in one direction, the *preconditions* for a move the other way are in place. (Some people put it more simply: If everybody thinks something, they're always wrong. This is a gross oversimplification, but most investors are indeed usually wrong at major turning points.)

Contrary opinion is a very useful tool to have because it keeps you from getting caught up in the prevailing market sentiment at major tops and bottoms.

This goes back to what I said earlier: Most people are bearish at market bottoms and bullish at market tops because that's what the prevailing trend is and where the news background is. But a real market bottom is a time to act optimistically—a time to buy. And a real market top is a time to act pessimistically—a time to sell.

The big risk with contrarian investing is that you'll be too early. This has dangers at both the bottom and the top. Bottoms, as I have said, can see the market lurch downward well beyond "normal" stopping points. And tops can see the market go up longer than anyone thinks it will as individual investors get caught up in the frenzy and buy quite late in the cycle.

Edwin Stern said it best, as quoted by Burton Crane in *The Sophisticated Investor* (1959):

"When everyone is bearish, everybody is apt to be wrong. When everybody is bullish, everybody may be right now and then."

It's even possible to take the concept of contrary opinion a step further, as I have through my *law of perversity*: "The market will do whatever it has to do to embarrass the greatest number of investors to the greatest extent possible."

Finally, remember this interesting tidbit:

If there are only 100 investors in the world, and 99 of them are bearish, and then one of them turns bullish, 98 percent of all investors still will be bearish—but the market will go up!

So find out what everyone thinks—and then start to consider whether it's time to go contrary to the prevailing sentiment. Never get yourself caught up in the prevailing sentiment wisdom without knowing exactly why you're doing so—and realizing that you always must consider the contrary viewpoint.

PART III

CHARTING TECHNIQUES AND PATTERNS

CHAPTER 6

THE IMPORTANCE OF CHARTS—A VISUAL CONFLUENCE OF PRICE, TIME, AND EMOTION

Why Charts?

Which conveys more information about a specific oak tree, a picture of the tree or a 1,000-word description? Now suppose that you have just five seconds to assimilate the information.

According to an old Chinese proverb, a picture is worth 1,000 words. To which I add: A chart is worth 1,000 numbers. A chart takes a jumble of numbers and makes them workable, and your mind makes visual connections that are not apparent in a list of numbers.

Remember, the primary number to chart is *stock price*, which is in constant flux. Each price is set where the supply and demand lines meet, where willing buyers meet willing sellers. Each time a buyer and a seller meet, the price can be different from the last. It can go up and go down. You track that change in price—that junction of supply and demand.

So the static number—the price on any given day—is not as important as the direction and rate of change. And charts let you understand them much, much more easily than looking at a list of numbers.

When charting, always remember two things: KISS and the 90/10 rule. KISS, of course, stands for "Keep It Simple, Stupid." The 90/10 rule, meanwhile, states that you can get 90 percent of the information from something in about 10 percent of the time, but it takes the remaining 90 percent of the time to get the remaining 10 percent of the information.

A Basic Chart

Before we go any further, let's define the elements of a basic chart. Figure 6-1 is a daily chart that shows the emerging-markets exchange-traded fund (EEM) from July 2008 through April 2009 and is from the invaluable DecisionPoint.com site that I use regularly.

The most basic thing on the chart, of course, is the price itself. Since this is a daily chart, each vertical line or bar depicts the trading for a particular day. The high and low prices each day are connected with a vertical line, and the closing price is represented by a little cross-tick.

The solid line on the price chart is a moving average. This one happens to be a 50-day exponentially smoothed moving average, but there are many, many different moving averages in use among market technicians. Moving averages are used

Figure 6-1: A Basic Chart.

Chart courtesy of DecisionPoint.com

to measure both trends and momentum. If the stock price is above its moving average, it's in an uptrend, and if it's below the moving average, it's in a downtrend. In addition, if the price is above the moving average and moving further and further above it, the stock is gaining momentum, whereas if the price is above the moving average but getting closer and closer to it, the stock is losing momentum.

The same works in reverse, of course, when the stock is below the moving average. In addition, if the stock price is way, way above the moving average (over 30 percent, let's say), it's overbought—extended on the upside—which makes it vulnerable to at least a short-term correction. The opposite is true if it's way, way below the moving average (as EEM was in October and November of 2008). And obviously, the longer term the moving average, the longer term is the trend you're measuring.

Finally, the line at the bottom of the chart is the all-important relative-strength line—which is simply the stock price divided by a broad market index such as the Standard & Poor's 500 Index (S&P 500).

Interpreting the relative-strength line is simple: A rising line means that the stock is outperforming the market; a falling price means that it isn't. Don't worry about the "price" of the relative-strength line; it means nothing. All we're interested in is whether the line is going up or going down.

(One of the greatest advantages of the DecisionPoint.com site, by the way, is that it enables you to easily chart a stock's relative strength versus just about anything—a market sector, an overseas stock market, and gold, to cite just a few examples, not just the S&P 500.)

There are, of course, all sorts of additional indicators and different methods of charting stocks that are available on the various charting websites. In this book, though, I'm not going to go beyond the basics—which is really all that long-term investors need—but if you'd like to learn more, see the Appendix for a few suggested resources. You'll also find a list of some of the better charting websites where you can look at individual stock charts to your heart's content.

Analyzing the Chart

We really need to determine just four things from stock charts:

1. Is the stock price going up or down?
2. Is the stock price gaining or losing momentum?
3. Is the stock overbought (extended on the upside) or oversold (extended on the downside)?
4. Is the stock's relative-strength line going up or down?

The EEM chart happens to reflect the best of all possible worlds.

1. The stock is going up; the price is above the moving average.
2. The stock is gaining momentum; the price is moving further and further above the moving average.
3. The stock is not yet overbought; the price isn't all that far above the moving average.
4. The stock is generating relative strength; the line at the bottom of the chart has been going up since October. (And the fact that EEM generated relative strength throughout the market's bottoming process was the tipoff that it was destined to be a market leader afterwards, as you'll see later.)

Please note that it takes virtually no time at all for you to determine these four points, which is all that you really need to be aware of as a long-term technically savvy investor. The 90/10 rule rules!

I am also happy to be able to report that the best of all possible worlds worked out very, very nicely for investors. EEM, which was 28.14 when this chart ended in April of 2009, hit a high of 44.02 in April 2010 and sold at 50.43 in May of 2011.

Lessons from a Basic Long-Term Chart—McDonald's

Figure 6-2 is one of my all-time favorite charts—an 11-year chart of McDonald's from 1970 to 1981 from the Securities Research Corporation's *Blue Book*. It illustrates the basic chart concepts very clearly, especially relative strength. Even more important, it highlights the importance of sentiment in predicting future stock prices.

To fully understand this chart, some background is necessary.

The big investing fad in the early 1970s was predictable consumer growth stocks. At that time, the United States was going through a time of unusually high inflation and unusually high interest rates, so companies found it difficult to borrow and expand. But approximately 50 giant consumer-goods companies were growing so fast that they generated their own cash needs and could finance themselves internally, so they didn't have to go to the capital markets to raise operating cash.

They were "fortresses in an angry sea." The inflationary seas were raging around them, but these companies were so strong that they could withstand the angry seas and still do nicely.

This group became known as the "Nifty Fifty," and McDonald's was a leader among them.

McDonald's growth rate was phenomenal! It was 25 percent per year compounded. And that growth rate was steady and unbroken throughout the decade. The "Nifty Fifty" investors foresaw this in 1973 (three years into the chart) and paid 75 times earnings for the stock. And Putnam, where I headed the Market Analysis Department, was one of the biggest of the "Nifty Fifty" investors.

Figure 6-2: McDonald's as a "Nifty Fifty" Stock.

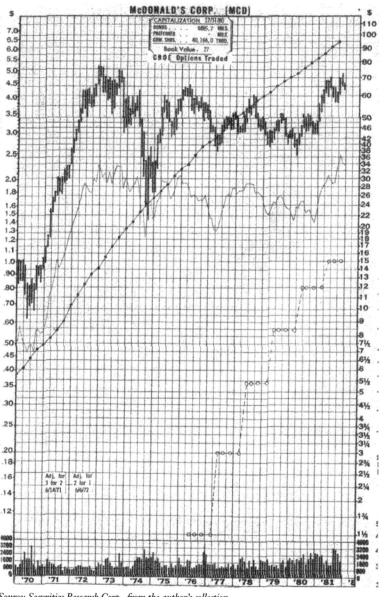

Source: Securities Research Corp., from the author's collection.

In 1973, every kind of fundamental analysis indicated that the stock price would go even higher.

But look carefully at the chart to see where McDonald's stock price actually went. (The earnings line is plotted on a scale such that if the price line is at the earnings line, the stock is selling at 15 times earnings. If the price line is above the earnings line, the stock is selling at more than 15 times earnings. If it is below, it is selling at below 15 times earnings.)

McDonald's stock price went from a high extreme of 75 times earnings in 1973 to a low extreme of 7.5 times earnings in 1980.

Well, 75 times earnings was, and is, a lot to pay for even a predictable growth stock. But the most stunning thing on the chart is that as the period of enthusiasm gave way to a corrective process, the price/earnings ratio of McDonald's plummeted from 75 times earnings to 7.5 times earnings *even though the company's compounded earnings growth rate was 25 percent throughout the period and it never missed a quarter.*

At Putnam, the fundamentally oriented money managers were driven to tears. They had analyzed the company and correctly forseen very good things. And those good things all came to pass: Every quarter, McDonald's earnings would come in at the expected 25 percent growth rate.

But the stock didn't do well. And it didn't do well quarter after quarter after quarter, despite those fabulous earnings. Why?

Here's what happened:

In 1973, McDonald's stock price increase had been driven by euphoria, by a recognition of future earnings. This euphoria pushed the stock price to an extreme valuation.

But once the emotional peak was reached, in 1973, the stock was all done. Basically, the market said, "Hey, McDonald's, you're a great company; you are going to do fabulously well over the next seven years. But, at 75 times earnings, I've already anticipated that and paid for it, and I'm not going to pay more."

And so the stock price stopped going up.

After that, the only question was, How low was it going to go?

If in 1973 I had predicted that all the analysts' earnings and growth forecasts for the next seven years would come true and that McDonald's, as a company, would do everything anyone expected and more, but despite that, its stock price would be lower in 1980 that it was in 1973, I would have been considered a lunatic.

But that's what happened.

McDonald's was unusually high priced at even 60 times earnings. When it went to 75 times earnings, the risk was even higher. Investors, of course, can never know ahead of time exactly when risk will be perceived as too much. At some point, though, the risk levels become high enough that the stock is going to respond. So all a technical analyst can do with these long-term charts is to say that risk levels are high or risk levels are low and that the stock is in a position to respond negatively to high-risk levels or is in a position to respond positively to low-risk levels. Predicting exactly when this will happen, though, is impossible. (John Maynard Keynes may have said it best: "Successful investing is anticipating the anticipation of others.") But this gives you a long-term perspective, whether you are in an enthusiastic period, where risk is way higher than usual, or you are in a period of pessimism, where risk is lower than usual.

McDonald's actually turned out to be a happier case than most. Its stock price was buoyed more than usual because its earnings kept growing. In a more normal situation, earnings would have been more sideways, and the price would have been biased to the downside.

So the price didn't go down much. But it didn't go up either, and people were not paying Putnam to own stocks whose prices went sideways—especially since a lot of other stocks were going up during that time. Our competitors thus got busy soliciting our clients and told them that Putnam has McDonald's and it has gone sideways over the last few years, and your account has gone sideways, whereas in our account we have bought such things as US Steel at five times earnings, and it is now at eight times earnings. And our accounts are going up.

But was McDonald's a bad purchase? It needn't have been, not with some sensible longer-term timing and planning. During its heyday, McDonald's went from 9 $1/4$ to 75 over a period of 2 $1/2$ years—and I can assure you that there were some down days, some minor corrections, along the way. But the stock price generally went up because investors anticipated great earnings. The trick is to spot when the price stops going up based on anticipation and it's time to sell. Remember: No stock's performance ever exactly tracks the performance of the underlying company. And no stock goes up forever, no matter what the company's earnings do.

And if the stock price is no longer going up, you have to accept that it is going down and not try to get back into it every time there is a little upside correction. Keep your eye on the long-term movements.

And what were things like at Putnam when McDonald's finally bottomed? You'll never guess: The following is the transcript of an interoffice memorandum exactly as it appeared at Putnam in 1980.

Anecdote—The Wall Street Week Memo

INTEROFFICE MEMORANDUM

TO: Norton H. Reamer, Martin M. Hale,
        J. David Wimberly, and Michael C. Hewitt

FROM: Walter R. Deemer   DATE: February 13, 1980

GROWTH STOCKS

As you know, I think that the big growth stocks are very attractive technically, with most of them apparently in the final phases of major reversal patterns. I also think that when the long-delayed recession finally hits that their earnings gains during a period of generally declining profits will make them stand out like "beacons in the night."

Two of the most obvious, at least to me, are McDonald's and Philip Morris, (which presently happen to be selling at 9 and 8 times trailing earnings, respectively) and I thought that it might be nice to mention them on the Wall Street Week program if the subject should come up. However, on checking with the Advisory Company, I was told I couldn't--they have sell programs underway presently in both stocks.

If this isn't a major buy signal for growth stocks, I don't know what is; the stocks are apparently being sold because of their disappointing price performance, but from a technical point of view, I think it's wrong to sell them now.

WRD

/ls

Anecdote—The Story of Baxter, US Steel, and John Maurice

This is from a special report I wrote and published on April 9, 1999:

Back in the Good Old Days at Putnam (circa 1973), when the Nifty Fifty were the only game in town and the Putnam Advisory Company—which was every bit as big a Nifty Fifty player as J. P. Morgan's Carl Hathaway, who got all the media coverage—was bringing in new accounts almost daily, the advisory managers used to make regular trips to the trading room to deliver a stack of buy tickets for their Core List stocks and a stack of sell tickets for the stocks they had inherited.

One afternoon, John Maurice, the manager of the Putnam Growth Fund, a card-carrying contrarian and one of the best and most astute money managers I have ever worked with, looked at the advisory manager who had just brought in that day's stack of buy and sell tickets and said, "Do you mind if I ask you something?"

"Sure."

"Do you ever wonder if US Steel, which you're selling at five times earnings, might possibly be a better stock than Baxter, which you're buying at 50 times earnings?"

"No," came the instant reply. "We were sold to our new client as a growth stock manager, and a growth stock manager we shall be."

But the deeply depressed US Steel *was* a better stock to buy in 1973 than the immensely exploited Baxter. Not only that, the money that came flooding into Putnam in 1973 and 1974 because of the sensational past performance of high-quality growth stocks left just as quickly toward the end of that decade, due to the underperformance of those growth stocks.

One final note: When I told this story in Boston, someone reminded me that the "Nifty Fifty" performance, which crested in 1973, caused John Neff, the highly regarded "value" manager of Vanguard's Windsor Fund, to come within one quarter of being fired at the time. Neff stuck to his style of investing, though, and his fund subsequently performed so well and got so big that it had to be closed to new investors 15 years later. Carl Hathaway's did not.

CHAPTER 7

SOME IMPORTANT LONG-TERM CHARTS

Long-Term Charts

You Claim That Technical Analysts Can Never Have Too Much Data. How Far Back Does Your Earliest Data Go?

My long-term charts go back as far as I can take them—sometimes as far back as 1870. I'm fascinated by the messages these long-term charts can give me. But there are charts in Fidelity's legendary chart room that go back even further than that. Fidelity has a chart of the stock market that goes all the way back to 1789. And, of course, there are data sets in Europe that go back into the 1500s that show long-term interest rates and so on.

But How Do You Keep the Data Constant? Don't Things Change Drastically from Decade to Decade?

I think that the fear of this is what keeps many investors from using longer-term charts. But it's overblown.

Remember, a stock market chart reflects primarily change over time, change to one number, whether it is the price of a single stock or the Standard & Poor's 500 Index (S&P 500). Numbers only go up or down, reflecting optimism or pessimism.

Having said that, there are ways to adjust charts so that they more accurately reflect long-term historic changes. We can do so in three ways:

1. Compare the rates of change to the number immediately preceding it.
2. Compare ratios of things that have stayed in approximately the same relation to each other, such as price versus earnings.
3. Compare ratios of price to a more fixed constant, such as gold or the median home.

Log Scales versus Arithmetic Scales on Long-Term Charts

When you look at long-term price charts, I can't emphasize enough that you must—must—use a log scale. With log scales, equal-percentage changes are shown as equal moves on the chart. So a stock that doubles from 1 to 2 and then from 2 to 4 has made two equal moves on the chart.

I can best show you why a log scale is essential on a long-term chart with the following two charts that my friend, Ron Griess, proprietor of Thechartstore.com, created especially for this book (Figures 7-1 and 7-2). Both of them show exactly the same thing—the Dow Jones Industrial Average (DJIA)

Figure 7-1: Dow Jones Industrial Average, 1870–Present, Nonlog Scale.

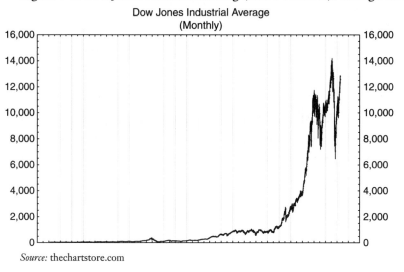

Source: thechartstore.com

Figure 7-2: Dow Jones Industrial Average, 1870–Present, Log Scale.

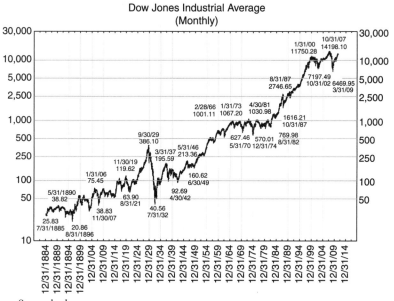

Source: thechartstore.com

from 1870 to the present—but one is plotted on an arithmetic scale and the other is on a log scale. As you'll see, they give dramatically different pictures of the very same thing.

The first chart, on the arithmetic scale (Figure 7-1), seems to show that the DJIA was doing nothing from 1870 until the 1950s and didn't really gain value until the 1990s.

But then look at the log chart (Figure 7-2), which accurately shows a much steadier growth over time. The numbers are the same, but the vertical scale on the chart now reflects the percentage changes rather than the price changes. The log scale clearly shows the DJIA's dramatic slump following the 1929 crash and two periods of above-average growth during the postwar period until about 1964 and from about 1984 to 1999. You simply can't get this information from a chart with an arithmetic scale.

S&P 500 from 1870 to the Present

We can get another wonderful long-term perspective from Figure 7-3, showing (on a log scale) the S&P 500 from 1870 to the present.

This chart shows several interesting things. First, true secular bull markets, where the price rises and keeps rising for a decade or more, happen only about 40 percent of the time. During the other 60 percent of the time, markets are range-bound. Sometimes range-bound markets have big up and down moves, but go generally sideways. At other times range-bound markets give back just about all their increases from the prior secular bull market. The chart shows five true secular bull markets together with the spans in between them

Figure 7-3: S&P 500, 1870–Present, Showing Structural Moves.

Home On The Range ... Secular Bull Markets are Rare Events

that last from 16 to 21 years, where the market moves up and down but essentially goes sideways.

The message from this chart: We are in one such generally sideways period now that started in October 2000. Just by analyzing this chart, then, we can infer that the S&P 500 will not start another secular bull market until between 2016 and 2021. In the meantime, of course, there will be shorter-term gains to be picked up, but investors will have to time their purchases and sales much more carefully than they do during a secular bull market.

Ratios—S&P 500 Since 1870

Price/Earnings (P/E) Ratio

Investors like to think that the stock they buy reflects the earning capacity of a company. When investors are pessimistic, P/E ratios tend to be very low. When they are optimistic, when they see (or at least think they see) growth ahead, P/E ratios can get absurdly high. So looking at the current P/E ratio and comparing it with its historical range can help you to determine whether the stock—or the market—is cheap, expensive, or somewhere in between.

Figure 7-4 shows the S&P 500 on a log scale, and Figure 7-5 shows Generally Accepted Accounting Principles (GAAP) earnings, also on a log scale. Figure 7-6 shows the ratio of price to prior peak earnings. The two bands show that for most of those 140 years, the ratio ranged between multiples of 8 and 20 times.

Figures 7-4, 7-5, 7-6, and 7-7: S&P 500, 1870–Present, to Compare with Other Charts.

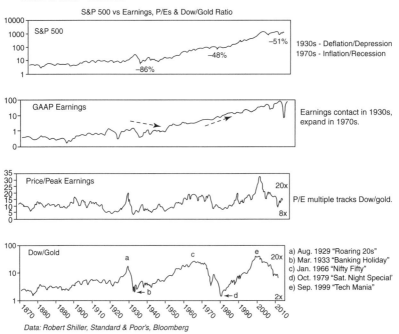

Data: Robert Shiller, Standard & Poor's, Bloomberg

Notice that sometimes stock prices got ahead of themselves and thus were in a high-risk area, and sometimes they got behind themselves, which is where the long-term opportunities come in.

In the late 1960s, we had enthusiasm, the "go-go" years, when stocks sold at very high valuations. Growth stocks and performance investing were all the rage. And then we went through a "secular revaluation process" (to use Fullermoney's David Fuller's wonderful phrase) that lasted until 1982. We gradually crawled out of that, and then there was the tech mania, and stocks went to absurd, bubble-like valuations.

Stock prices are now correcting to more normal valuation levels. But they haven't gotten back to their long-term trend lines. This suggests that we are probably in the midst of a corrective process rather than at the end of it.

You can't analyze P/E ratios exactly; you can only know whether in general they are relatively high or relatively low. Five is very low. Twenty-five is very high. Where we are now is in the middle. And that's about all the information you can squeeze from the P/E ratio—that it is roughly in the middle of its historic range.

Figure 7-7 shows the ratio of the DJIA to the price of gold.

Notice that this chart tracks the price-to-peak-earnings ratio of the chart shown in Figure 7-6.

Gold is the one thing thought to be somewhat interchangeable with money. It is in limited quantity, and it has almost no industrial uses. Its price was pegged to the dollar from 1945 to 1971 and has been floating since then. Some people use the price of gold to establish an approximate rate of monetary inflation.

But it would be more appropriate to say that the price of gold reflects confidence in the future direction of our currency. Rising prices indicate a belief that monetary inflation will continue or accelerate or that the dollar will lose value. Falling prices indicate a belief that monetary inflation will be contained or even that there will be deflation or that the dollar will increase in value.

I also have included a chart that shows a ratio not usually seen: home prices to gold (Figure 7-8). This shows that at the time the chart was compiled in 2011, it took 120 ounces of gold to buy the median house. Back in 1980, the median house cost 102 ounces of gold.

The median home has changed since then. It is larger and has more amenities. But we are also coming out of a bubble in home prices.

So, in gold terms, is housing now cheap? Or is gold in a bubble? It's impossible to tell. But we can see that house prices are trending downward relative to the price of gold.

In addition, houses are now selling below replacement cost in many cases. But residential real estate has some secular excesses to finish working off, as you'll see in Chapter 19.

Figure 7-8: Home/Gold Price Ratios.

Should Numbers Be Adjusted for Inflation?

Many investors assume that dollar amounts should be adjusted for inflation. But what type of inflation, and who defines it?

There are several different types of inflation. There is "real" inflation, where the price of a commodity goes up permanently (this happens when the commodity itself is increasingly scarce, when the means of creating it becomes more expensive, or when more people demand it). There is also monetary inflation, and this is where, all other things being equal, the value of money goes down. This usually occurs when there is too much money in circulation.

The government's measure of inflation is imperfect and is also changeable at political will. Right now their "core" measure of inflation exempts changes to the price of oil and food, where rising prices are assumed to be caused by temporary shortages. (As wags point out, the Consumer Price Index is a terrific measure of inflation for people who don't eat, don't drive, and don't heat their homes.)

I'm not saying that inflation-adjusted numbers have no value at all. They do. Just be forewarned that they are far from precise.

CHAPTER 8

MEANS AND MEAN REVERSION

Once you have a good base number set—whether that set is a simple dollar price or some sort of a ratio—one way to put the data into long-term perspective is with a mean, or arithmetical average.

The mean is simply the average of the data for a certain period of time. Figure 8-1 shows price to prior peak earnings from 1870 to September 2011, with the simplest mean line imaginable. Half the data points are above the line, and half below it.

With the exception of a short blip in 2008, we have been above the mean line almost continuously since the mid-1980s. Even since the 1950s, there have been more data points above the line than below it. This suggests that there may be a correction—or *mean reversion*—ahead.

(See also the Home-on-the-Range chart in Figure 7-3.)

The length of time above the mean also may suggest a more fundamental shift—and one that investors need to be aware of.

Stocks have become a more "popular" investment, and here's one reason for it:

Figure 8-1: Standard & Poor's 500 Index (S&P 500) Price to Prior Peak Earnings With Mean Line, 1870–Present.

Years ago, most individuals invested in themselves first. Back 150 years ago, they probably bought farmland. Later, they started a store, a tiny factory, or a service station.

Back then, the stock market was nothing more than a rich man's playground.

But gradually, very gradually, more and more workers gravitated toward paid employment by a third party, and "investments" went not to the businesses that people owned but to bets on the performance of third parties. At first, it was fixed-income investments, investments that generated a small but sure income, such as a savings account or equivalent. Or maybe it was a non-income-producing investment, such as buying a home, fixing it up, living in it, and hoping that the price would rise.

Even in the early 1960s, the rate of public participation in the stock market was still low because stocks were expensive relative to salaries. And there were other kinds of investments: savings accounts that offered modest but real returns, house prices that appreciated, and so forth. But now those same investments offer little or uncertain returns.

And many more "average Joe" investors are desperate to save up for a long, expensive retirement.

Hence equities.

The average investor has gone from investing in himself to making an investment in something over which he has no control and little knowledge. And he chases the highest-return but highest-risk class of investment, the lowest claim in bankruptcy—equities.

So back to the chart.

Chasing high price/earnings (P/E) ratio stocks indicates an enthusiasm for stocks, but that enthusiasm may be propelled by a lack of credible alternatives, especially among small investors, whose alternative assets would include their family home and a savings account, neither of which has attractive rates of return at the moment.

In fact, stock prices may have become an alternate currency, in some cases, with more people parking shorter-term money there rather than in a bank.

On the other hand, too many desperate investors may be chasing too few credible stocks, causing a long-term inflation in stock prices.

It's something to think about.

Definition—Regression to the Mean/Mean Reversion

The mean is nothing more than an average, a constantly changing number that reflects a mathematical point where there are an equal number of data points above and below the calculated number.

Many analysts say that the market ultimately "reverts to the mean" as if the mean had some kind of magnetic attraction; where the market should be. But the market hardly ever stops at the mean. It oscillates between extremes of fear on the downside and greed on the upside, and it rarely stops right at the mean. The market always swings like a pendulum from periods of pessimism to periods of optimism, and it is always prone to extremes at both ends. Investors should be worried much more about how far the pendulum will swing than where the mean is.

Let's say, using round numbers, that the P/E ratio is in a range between 5 and 25. So the mean is 15. So let's say that the P/E ratio peaked at 25 but is now 15. Voilà. Should we be happy? No. If the P/E ratio stopped when it got to 15, then the mean wouldn't be 15. The extremes would be 25 and 15, and the mean would be 20. For the mean to be 15, there have to be as many data points below the mean as above it.

The scary thing about this is that analysts are always reassuring people when the market has regressed or returned to the mean. But the mean is meaningless in assessing stock prices. Stock prices are what they are on any given day. They do not respect mathematical calculations of where they should hang around in the middle. In fact, they are likely to be moving quickly in one direction or the other.

This is very important to consider today.

During the 1990s, valuations were above average, and returns were outsized. During 2000 to 2010, valuations have been correcting toward more normal rates of return but have not yet reached the other extreme.

People say, "Aha! We have regressed to the mean." And what they think they are saying is that valuations are now reasonable, and the implication is that they could stay that way.

These people couldn't be more wrong.

At this particular time, having gone through a period of extreme optimism in the 1990s, the issue is, How far is the pendulum likely to swing the other way? History suggests that it is likely to swing, eventually, to a period of pessimism and that since the 2000–2007 period, the general public investor, as opposed to hedge fund traders, high-frequency computers, and so on, has become less and less enchanted with stocks. Even though the market has been doing reasonably well since 2009, the numbers suggest that the equal but opposite extreme has yet to be seen.

Frank Peluso, my favorite cycles analyst, has compared market cycles to the swings of a pendulum. The market starts down, accelerates, reaches its maximum point of acceleration, then decelerates, and finally ends at an extreme on the other side.

So the concept of cycle analysis is this: Where is the pendulum in its arc? Is it accelerating or decelerating? Frank applied the same methodology to stock prices.

Figure 8-2: S&P 500 Long-Term Inflation-Adjusted Real Growth Since 1871 on a Log Scale.

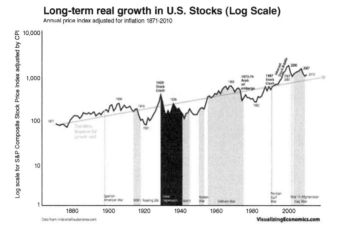

The mean, though, lies somewhere near the point of maximum acceleration. If you think about that for a while, you'll understand why the mean is not the magic stopping place that Wall Street strategists would have you think it is.

I published the chart in Figure 8-2 showing long-term real growth and stock prices early in 2011. It's another reversion-to-the-mean chart; it shows you not only the peaks and troughs but also the least-squares trend line and how stock prices oscillate around that. (A *least-squares trend line* is the straight line for which the sum of the squares of the deviations is minimized and is used instead of the mean when the data generally are rising or falling rather than flat.) Here, too, the takeaway is that the least-squares trend line is a midpoint—not a stopping place.

Relative-Strength Line

Basically, you want to own a stock that's doing two things: (1) going up (the price on the stock chart) and (2) going up more than the market (the relative-strength line on the chart). David Keller, managing director of research for Fidelity Investments in Boston and the person who manages Fidelity's technical analysis team, said during a Boston Society of Security Analysts presentation in 2010 that "I never look at a chart that doesn't have a relative-strength line on it." I don't either; it's that important!

Relative-strength lines can show the stock versus either the broad market or a sector grouping. Naturally, the more restrictive the grouping, the closer the relative-strength line will track the stock.

Momentum Measures/Oscillators

Some technicians use a dizzying array of momentum measures and oscillators to verify or refute one another, but you really need only one of each to know what's going on with the momentum and overbought/oversold situations.

Momentum is the speed at which prices (or other data) are changing—the rate of change of the data, if you will. If a stock is gaining momentum, it is going up at a faster rate than before, and if it is losing momentum, it's going up at a slower rate. *Overbought* and *oversold*, meanwhile, are terms that refer to whether a stock has gone up or down too much too fast and is probably due for some sort of corrective move. Finally, an oscillator is simply the plot of the difference between the price (or some other data point) and either a previous price or a moving average; the higher the oscillator, the further above the previous price or moving average is the current price or data point.

As an example, I'll use a 20-day trading period, which is approximately a month. If you chart the rate of change of a stock price over a 20-day period—a 20-day oscillator—you will find that it peaks at the very beginning of a bull market because prices go up most rapidly at the very beginning of a bull market. Gradually, the price goes up less and less rapidly, and your oscillator's line will work gradually lower. At some point, it will fall to zero, which tells you that the price has stopped going up and is now going sideways. And the oscillator then will continue going lower until, at the end of the bear market, it will be at its most negative level.

An oscillator thus tends to go from the maximum low at the end of a bear market to the maximum high at the beginning of a bull market; then work its way gradually lower until the end of the next bear market. The problem in a bear market, of course, is knowing where that maximum low is because things always can get worse than you think. People who say "The market has gone down so much, it's got to be a buy" always can get caught by the fact that the market can go down even farther and be even more of a buy. This is what happened in 2008. So, although you can use an oscillator to tell you that prices have gone down at a rate similar to the rate they declined at the end of the last bear market, you can't use it to pinpoint the end of the bear market. Low oscillator readings simply mean that one precondition for the bear market being over has been met, and it is time to be looking for a bear market bottom—even if such a bottom does not materialize at that particular hour.

MEANS AND MEAN REVERSION

On the flip side, meanwhile, looking at how high the oscillator gets at the beginning of a move will tell you how strong
and how durable the move is. If the advance is extraordinarily
powerful, it generates what I call *breakaway momentum*, which
I'll discuss in just a minute.

There are literally hundreds of oscillators in use among the
technical fraternity, and discussing the differences between
them and their myriad interpretations is beyond the scope of
this book. (If you're interested in learning more about oscillators, the Appendix has a number of suggestions for you.)
All that long-term investors really need to know, though, are
(1) Is the stock's price gaining or losing momentum? and (2)
Is the stock's price overbought or oversold?

(Remember the 90/10 rule!)

Breakaway Momentum

Downside momentum usually peaks at the end of a decline
as prices cascade into a primary low. On the upside, though,
momentum peaks at the beginning of an advance and then dissipates gradually as the advance goes on, and the more powerful the momentum at the move's beginning, the stronger is
the overall move. *Really* strong momentum is found only at
the beginning of a *really* strong move—a new bull market or
a new intermediate up-leg within a bull market. I coined the
term *breakaway momentum* in the 1970s to describe this really
powerful upside momentum.

Breakaway momentum (some people call it a *breadth thrust*)
occurs when 10-day total advances on the New York Stock

Table 8-1: Breakaway Momentum Since 1945

Date	A/D Ratio	Date	A/D Ratio
July 14, 1949	2.07	January 14, 1976	2.53
November 20, 1950	2.01	August 26, 1982	2.68
January 26, 1954	2.01	October 13, 1982	2.09
January 24, 1958	2.00	January 23, 1985	1.972
July 12, 1962	2.37	January 15, 1987	2.36
November 12, 1962	2.50	February 5, 1991	2.17
January 18, 1967	2.13	January 6, 1992	1.974
December 7, 1970	2.12	March 23, 2009	2.22
December 8, 1971	1.98	July 23, 2009	2.17
January 14, 1975	2.46	September 16, 2009	2.32

Exchange (NYSE) are greater than 1.97 times 10-day total NYSE declines. It is a relatively uncommon phenomenon; Table 8-1 shows the 20 times this has occurred since World War II (an average of once every 3½ years).

How is breakaway momentum typically achieved? It's not easy. Usually, three things have to happen. First, we need a very strong advance at the outset of the 10-day period. Typically, this requires an advance/decline (A/D) ratio in the area of 2,800 to 500 on the first day, 2,500 to 700 on day 2, and 2,050 to 1,050 on days 3 and 4. This creates a cumulative ratio of 2.69 to 1, which is well above the 1.97 threshold. The very strong advances on the first two days followed by still-positive breadth on the next two days are a formidable achievement, but the next one is even tougher. Markets never go straight up, and *the real trick in achieving breakaway momentum is to keep declines limited during the inevitable corrections that occur in any 10-day period.* In order to keep declines limited during corrections, the corrections must be minimal; often this occurs when intraday declines abort before the close, and a big-breadth deficit turns into just a narrow one by day's end. Breadth during the "correction days" (days 5 and 6), then, should be no worse than 1,400 to 1,700. Although this pushes the cumulative ratio down to 1.84, this is a far from insurmountable deficit. The final element needed to get breakaway momentum is a second strong advance during days 7 through 10—not quite as strong as the initial advance but not too far behind it either. If, for example, the market generates breadth during days 7 through 10 of 2,500 to 700, 2,300 to 800, 2,100 to 1,000, and 1,900 to 1,200, the 10-day breadth totals are 21,000 and 10,400. This generates a 10-day breadth ratio of 2.02—breakaway momentum!

The real trick in generating breakaway momentum, then, is not a lot of advances: *It's a lack of declines.* If the market stages a strong two-day advance, for example, it *must* maintain very positive breadth days for a couple of days afterward (days 3 and 4 and 9 and 10) to keep the 10-day declines to a minimum. Also, declines must be kept to a minimum during the "normal" correction in the middle of the 10-day period; declines can exceed advances during those two days, but not by much, or it will be impossible for the market to generate the two advances needed to offset every decline.

And just to illustrate the linkage between the economy and the stock market, which is a leading economic indicator: The stock market very often generates breakaway momentum three months before the end of a recession (as later determined by the National Bureau of Economic Research, the arbiter of such things).

Selling Climaxes

The stock market goes up the fastest at the beginning of a move—but it goes down the fastest at the end of a decline. This often results in what is called a *selling climax*, where prices fall more and more rapidly until they finally hit bottom and then rebound just as rapidly for a short time—all on extremely heavy volume. The market then tries to stabilize via a process called *testing the low* as the initial sharp but relatively short-lived rebound is followed by a series of lurches to the downside where the averages try to hold above the climactic low. The initial test usually occurs three to four days afterward, and a more thorough—and more traumatic—test often takes place three to four weeks afterward. If selling pressure, as measured by such things as volume and the number of new lows, does not exceed the level it reached during the selling climax, the test is likely to be successful; if not, the market hasn't reached its final bottom yet.

Tests of prior lows are extremely traumatic to live through. During the initial decline, investors watch numbly to see just how low the market will go, but during the testing process—when the news is inevitably at its worst—there is a great fear of "Here we go again." It is only when the market holds above its climactic low (or, in its perverse way, slightly undercuts it before reversing back to the upside, which happens a lot) that the fears can be laid to rest.

Figure 8-3: DJIA 1998 Bottom.

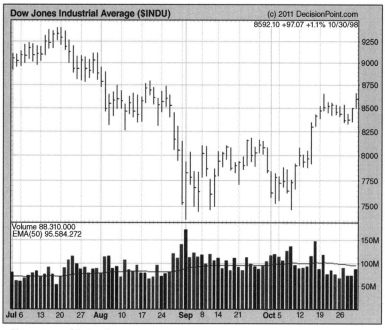

Chart courtesy of DecisionPoint.com

A successful testing process, in fact, is quite similar to what someone goes through after a big night of drinking: The initial low is equivalent to the first huge burst of vomiting, and subsequent lows are equivalent to lesser and lesser upchucks. Ideally, in fact, the testing process ends up with the market getting a case of the dry heaves: It retches and retches, but there's nothing left to come up.

Figure 8-3 is a chart of the 1998 bottom in the Dow Jones Industrial Average (DJIA) from DecisionPoint.com and is a very good illustration of a climactic low in the market and the subsequent testing process.

Caveat on Indexes

A lot of people think that the Standard & Poor's 500 Index (S&P 500), the reference index that virtually all professionals use, is a static index. They couldn't be more wrong! Indexes change over the years, and some of them change more than others. Most often they change to reflect fundamental changes. Big indexed companies merge and go out of business; tiny basement startups take off and become powerhouses that an index cannot ignore.

So, over time, an index may approximately reflect a representative group of the same types of companies. In the short run, though, the timing for exactly when companies are added or subtracted may create anomalies, and an index's price may be very misleading.

During the dot-com bubble, for example, the prices of tech stocks weren't the only thing that tanked. They took the S&P Index with them.

S&P noticed after some of the dot-com stocks had gone up a lot that they had gone up a lot. And so S&P added them to the S&P average only after they had already gone up a lot and were at exceedingly high prices. Yahoo!, to cite but one example, had gone from under a dollar in December 1996 to $87 in December 2009, when S&P added it to the S&P 500. It rose to $125 during the next three weeks and then slid all the way down to $4 in mid-2001. The problem, of course, was that the S&P 500 ended up getting virtually no benefit from the dot-com stock whatsoever on the way up; after Yahoo! (YHOO) was added to the index, it went up just another 38 points in three weeks. Then YHOO fell 121 points during the next year and a half—and the S&P 500 suffered through every single one of those 121 points on the way down.

Yahoo! was hardly the only dot-com stock that was added to the S&P 500 then, and those stocks ended up creating a horribly negative bias. Because the S&P 500 added a lot of dot-com stocks close to their peaks, the average had a much heavier dot-com weighting on the way down than it did on the way up.

This is why the S&P 500 can be very misleading. People tend to think of it as a static index—something that is etched in stone. But you may be surprised to learn how actively managed it is; S&P's stock selection committee made over 300 changes in the S&P 500 between 2000 and 2009.

There is another problem, too.

The S&P stock selection committee wields enormous power on Wall Street because every time it adds a stock to the index, all the index funds have to buy it. And every time S&P deletes a stock, the index funds have to sell it. And so, when S&P finally came around and decided that, in the case of the dot-com stocks, they were underrepresented after they had made a big run-up and added some of them to the S&P 500, the index funds were forced to buy the darn things even though they'd already gone so far up that no bona fide long-term investor would touch them with a 10-foot pole.

So the S&P 500 is not something that is etched in stone— not by a long shot! It changes quite a bit. And those changes often detract rather than add to the performance because S&P's stock selection committee very often is late in its selections; the committee reacts to moves that have already taken place. And so the stocks finally take on representation in the index after they have already had a move—after it is too late for them to help the S&P on the upside—but they still can make a big impact on it on the downside.

Anecdote—The Cathedral of Charts

I was very privileged a couple of years ago to be treated to a tour of Fidelity's chart room, the reference area for financial markets at one of the biggest institutional investors in the world (Figure 8-4). Displayed on the walls are charts of all kinds, from interest rates through overseas markets to a very long-term chart of the U.S. stock market going all the way back to 1779. (The latter chart has several pre-S&P and Dow Jones series, such as the Cleveland Trust Index, that have been spliced together. Intriguingly, the source of the pre-1832 data is labeled "Confidential Source," which has led me to all sorts of strange speculations with regard to the actual source. Was it a seance with someone from that era, a scroll from a tomb, or what?)

Only long-term charts are displayed in the chart room; no Elliott waves or stochastic oscillators there. In one area, charts of major U.S. groups dating from 1990 are grouped together; in another, charts of all overseas markets are similarly grouped. I found the effect to be truly inspirational—in every sense of the word. I couldn't help but get a very long-term perspective on the financial markets while quietly studying the charts, as a number of fund managers did during my visit. You find yourself contemplating them as you would contemplate great works in a museum. "Cathedral of Charts" alludes to one of the great wonders of the investing world and therefore is deeply respectful, not comedic, and the term *Chart Room* is capitalized intentionally.

Figure 8-4 shows a rare glimpse inside the "Cathedral of Charts" during one of my visits. I am deeply appreciative to David Keller, managing director of research for Fidelity Investments in Boston, shown in the picture with me, for giving me permission to include this picture in this book.

At the time of my visit in early 2010, I was struck by the incredible and unprecedented broadness of the global bull market that showed no signs of becoming more selective yet.

Figure 8-4: Walter Deemer Inside the "Cathedral of Charts."

As usual, though, life is not that simple, and I was reminded of one of the many great experiences I've had during my career. It was back when I spoke at the Conference on Technical Analysis in Cambridge, England, in mid-September 1974. My topic was the U.S. market; another speaker, David Fuller, addressed the British market, and a third covered every other market in the world. That third speaker was Adrian Shrikker, the media-dubbed "Chartist Pope," who followed the world's stock markets from his base in Luxemburg.

Mr. Shrikker showed us stock chart after stock chart in markets ranging from continental Europe all the way to the Pacific Rim. After this had gone on for quite a long time, a delegate finally raised his hand. "Mr. Shrikker, you have shown us a great many charts of stocks in downtrends. Could you now show us some stocks in an uptrend?"

Mr. Shrikker, who was not very tall in the first place, drew himself up to his full height and said, in forceful tones that I will never forget, "No . . . no, I cannot do that. There is no stock in the world that is in an uptrend!"

The six-year global bear market ended three weeks later.

(In fairness, I should say that some charts—and Mr. Shrikker—turned positive soon after the upcoming bottom. The moral thus may be that even though everything is bullish or bearish and therefore can't get any better or any worse, one must wait for the first signs of change before fading the unanimous evidence.)

PART IV

CYCLES AND WAVES

CHAPTER 9

MARKET-BASED CYCLES

Cycles are a very important part of a market analyst's tool-
box. A cycle is simply a relatively regularly occurring
move in a data series, and it's always measured from low to low
for reasons I'll discuss shortly. Every expansion cycle—whatever the cycle's length—ultimately creates excesses, whether in
the economy or in the stock market, that need to be corrected.
And that process, that contraction, ultimately leads to the next
expansion.

There are two cycles a technically savvy long-term investor needs to be aware of: the *four-year cycle*, where the stock
market makes an important low every four years or so, and
the *Kondratieff wave*, which is a very important but much less
clearly defined cycle where the stock market—as well as many
other financial series—makes generational lows every 50 years
or so. I'll discuss that first.

Long Cycles—The Kondratieff Wave

The longest documented financial cycle is the Kondratieff
wave, which is slightly over 50 years in length (Figure 9-1). It

Figure 9-1: Kondratieff Wave/Gold.

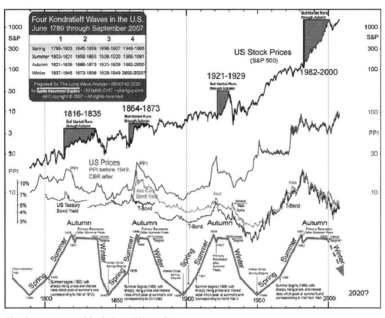

ChartGuy.com, prepared for the Long Wave Analyst

was developed in the 1930s by Nikolai Kondratieff, a Russian economist who had been asked by the Russian government to analyze the depression that was then taking place in the Western world. Kondratieff responded that the depression was part of a long-term cycle of boom and bust lasting approximately 54 years, that the West was at the bottom of its bust cycle, and that Western economies would soon recover.

When he reported this, he was sent to Siberia for glorifying decadent capitalism.

But he was right—because he said that there are long swings in psychology and sentiment from euphoria to despair and back again. Some analysts, in fact, break them down into seasons: The long swing up is the *Kondratieff spring*, the peak is the *Kondratieff summer*, the decline is the *Kondratieff autumn*, and the bottoming process is the *Kondratieff winter*. We Americans had a period of euphoria in the 1920s, and we had a period of despair in the 1930s and 1940s. And, just as spring and summer always follow winter, we swung back to euphoria starting in the 1950s.

According to the Kondratieff cycle, we have just worked our way through an extended period of global euphoria, with Japan peaking at the end of 1989 and the United States peaking in 2007. And we are now in the inevitable downswing that follows. This will be accompanied by a period of cooling off and debt contraction and ultimately will set the foundations for another great upswing in the economy and financial markets. Unfortunately, we have to get through the Kondratieff winter first.

A discussion of the characteristics of a Kondratieff winter and their implications for investors is beyond the scope of this book; if you're interested in pursuing this, I offer some suggestions for further reading in the Appendix. Suffice it to say that the corrective processes that got underway in earnest in the financial markets in 2007 are likely to continue for quite a while to come—which means that investors are going to have to work a lot harder than usual to make money consistently in the stock market.

One of the big problems with the Kondratieff cycle is that it can't be defined precisely. If it could be defined as a 52.3-year cycle, the academics might like it much better, but the Kondratieff cycle depends on psychology, not an exact sequence of events. As Bob Farrell has said, "History doesn't repeat itself exactly, but human behavior does."

The current Kondratieff cycle has been longer than usual. My own personal hypothesis is that the Kondratieff cycle measures things that occur over a period of two generations; it takes two generations to forget the mistakes of the past and repeat them. And with people living longer, the generations are lasting longer, and therefore, it takes people longer to forget the mistakes of the past and repeat them. I obviously can't prove this; all I'm saying here is that there is a somewhat indefinable but very real long-term swing in economic activity and investor enthusiasm from exuberance to despair and back to exuberance. Those swings take something like 54 years to go from one bottom to the next, and we're heading toward the next trough now.

Four-Year Cycle(s)

There are two widely followed four-year cycles in the stock market: the *four-year (Kitchin) cycle* and the *presidential cycle*. The two cycles have run somewhat parallel to each other over the years but have significant definitional differences. In my opinion, the four-year cycle is a real phenomenon, and the presidential cycle is not. I'm therefore going to discuss the four-year cycle first, using the latest charts available at the time this book went to press.

Although the two cycles have been tracking pretty closely together for many decades, they are now, as I write in August 2011, poised to make a major divergence.

(*Note:* Follow-up commentary will be available on the author's blog.)

The Four-Year (Kitchin) Cycle

The four-year cycle can be traced back to work done by Harvard's Joseph Kitchin in 1923 (Figure 9-2). Kitchin analyzed data that predated the establishment of the Federal Reserve in 1913 and also noted the presence of a four-year cycle in the United Kingdom late in the nineteenth century and early in the twentieth century, well before the two economies were linked as closely as they are today. The four-year cycle, in other words, was not based on either Federal Reserve actions or presidential elections. It simply states that the stock market makes a major low every four years or so. (Nobody calls this low the "Kitchin sink," and I can't imagine why not.)

The four-year-cycle lows may not represent much of a correction (as in 1994), but the low still will be the most important

Figure 9-2: Four-Year Cycle.

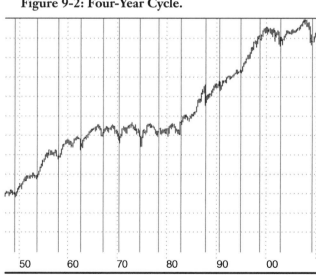

correction during that four-year period. It is the lowest low during that four-year cyle.

And notice that I said "or so." There is a tendency for the lows to occur at slightly more or less than four years. Also, very occasionally, the low gets pushed back, extending the four-year cycle into a fifth or sixth year, as we'll see in a minute.

The lows are regular. The peaks, however, are not regular at all and therefore can't be used for timing purposes. They can be early in the cycle (we call that a *skewed-left peak*) or late in the cycle (*skewed right*), and their positioning can produce important information.

If the underlying cycle is stronger than average (i.e., if we're in a secular bull market), the top usually will occur after the halfway point; it will be skewed to the right on the chart. If the underlying cycle is weaker than average, though, the four-year-cycle top usually will be made before the halfway point, and the cycle will be skewed to the left on the chart. By the same token, if you know that the underlying trend is stronger or weaker than average, you can anticipate that the cycle will peak after or before its halfway point.

If a cycle is skewed to the right or skewed to the left (i.e., if the top occurs before or after the halfway point), then it tells you a lot about the strength of the underlying trend (which I'll discuss in Chapter 12). By the same token, if you know that the underlying trend is stronger or weaker than average, you can anticipate that the cycle will peak after or before it's halfway point.

The four-year cycle is not exact but has been remarkably consistent. The stock market made major lows in 1949, 1953, 1957, 1962 (the 1961 low got pushed back a year), 1966 (which was four years after 1962 and thus put the market on a new four-year timetable), 1970, 1974, 1978, 1982, 1987 (the 1986 low got pushed back a year), 1990 (which put the market back on the old four-year timetable), 1994, 1998, and 2002.

In fact, over a very long period of time, both the presidential cycle (which I'll get to shortly) and the four-year cycle have been remarkably consistent. But both went out of whack in 2006. And that's both significant and unnerving; both cycles said that the stock market was supposed to make a major low in 2006, but the market didn't cooperate. It took two more years, until late 2008 and early 2009, for it to do so.

The presidential cycle, of course, just considers this as an anomaly and chugs on, tethered as it is to the election.

The four-year cycle is another story. It's missed lows before—but has always regained traction afterward and gone back to its regular pattern.

Bull Market Extensions and the Four-Year Cycle

There have been only three times in the past when the four-year-cycle low occurred more than four years after the prior low. All of them ended very badly.

> *1961–1962.* The stock market made a major low in October 1957, so the next low was scheduled for the fourth quarter of 1961. The market, however, made a high in December 1961 rather than a low. It paid the price afterward: The Dow Jones Industrial Average plunged from 725 in March 1962 to 560 at the end of May and bottomed

at 520 at the end of June. The decline became known as the "Crash of 1962," and those of us who lived through that extremely emotional decline will never forget it. (May 29, 1962, was the day when the New York Stock Exchange ticker ran so late that it didn't finish printing the day's transactions until after eight o'clock that night.)

1986–1987. The stock market made a major low in August 1982, so the next low was scheduled for mid-1986. The market, however, paused only briefly in 1986; the Dow then rallied from 1896 at the end of the year to 2746 the following August. It then plunged to 1616 in October, highlighted by a 22.6 percent implosion on Monday, October 19—the almost-unbelievable "Crash of 1987."

2006–2009. The stock market made a major low in October 2002, so the next low was scheduled for late 2006. The market, however, didn't even top out until October 2007—but the bloodbath that followed nearly brought the whole financial system down, not just the stock market.

Why do bull-market extensions end so badly? My guess is that the normal excesses that build up during a four-year-cycle advance build up much more than usual during the extensions. The subsequent bear markets thus have a lot more excesses than usual to correct. The real takeaway here, though, is that if the market doesn't make a four-year-cycle low when it's supposed to, this is not a sign of strength but rather a warning that structural excesses are building up that will have to be dealt with in the not too distant future.

Future of the Four-Year Cycle

The bottom line, though, is that over the long term, the four-year cycle has worked very, very well in the past, and there is no reason to believe that it won't continue to work in the future. Market sentiment is constantly swinging from enthusiasm to pessimism and back again. And, apparently, there is a four-year cycle that delineates how long these swings take, from a pessimistic low to an optimistic high and back again to a pessimistic low.

Four-year cycles, of course, take place within even longer-term trends. They're called *secular trends*, and they refer to moves in the stock market that persist over more than one four-year cycle that generate either higher and higher four-year-cycle highs or lower and lower four-year-cycle lows. The secular bull market that began in 1982, for instance, lasted over a number of four-year cycles. More recently, on the Nasdaq a secular corrective process (that is, a secular bear market) began in 2000 and still hasn't been totally completed.

The Presidential Cycle

Many people follow something called the *presidential cycle* in lieu of the four-year cycle. The presidential cycle, of course, follows the U.S. presidential term and is grounded in Machiavellian principles. According to market folklore, the president and the Federal Reserve conspire to stimulate the economy prior to a presidential election to ensure that economic conditions are the best they can possibly be on election day. The upbeat economy, in turn, then leads voters to award another term to the party in the White House because the incumbents are "obviously" responsible for those wonderful economic conditions. The overstimulation prior to the election then is followed by restrictive measures afterward that cool off the economy for two years and set up the next round of stimulus before the next presidential election. This all leads to the two preelection years being much better for the stock market than the two postelection years.

As it happens, this works out quite well historically. According to Ned Davis Research in Venice, Florida, the average return the year after a presidential election (the most recent such year was 2009) is 5.5 percent; it then falls to only 3.7 percent in the year after that (2010) when the restrictive measures are supposedly exacting their maximum toll. Then, as the political and economic masters of the universe start unleashing their magic, the average return rises to 12.6 percent in the preelection year (2011) and is a still good 7.5 percent in the election year itself (2012).

The problem, though, is that the presidential cycle said that 2009 and 2010 were not supposed to be good years, but they were—2009 especially. In addition, the Federal Reserve was stimulating like crazy in those two years. The question now is what is the Fed going to do to continue stimulating like crazy and keep the economy going so that the electorate will be wonderfully happy in 2012?

Federal Reserve stimulation can goose the markets, and it was undoubtedly responsible for at least some of the happy times in 2009 and 2010. But I doubt very much if, historically, the Fed always wants to get the party in power reelected. To me, this is a pretty far-fetched assumption.

The bottom line (as far as I'm concerned) is that the presidential cycle worked very nicely when it was lined up with the four-year cycle. Now that it isn't any more, it should be regarded with a great deal of suspicion.

Seasonal Cycles

"Sell in May and Go Away?"

There are all sorts of seasonal factors on Wall Street. I don't believe in them too much, though, because they're just not all that reliable. In 2010, for example, the traditional summer rally turned into a summer decline, and the traditional September–October decline turned into a September–October rally. So, sometimes seasonality works and sometimes it doesn't—especially when hedge funds see a seasonal move coming and front-run it. (I also was worried that if I stressed the seasonal factors at Putnam too much, one morning I would come in to find that I had been replaced by a calendar!)

Elliott Waves

Before I leave the subject of cycles, I probably should comment briefly on Elliott wave analysis, which is very popular in some circles. Many investors, in fact, swear by the Elliott wave theory, a complex and ultimately befuddling (to me) methodology that is explained in a host of interesting books that many investors love to try to decipher.

I've never had a lot of success with Elliott waves, though, except in hindsight.

In a very broad sense, Elliott waves make sense, in that a major move is often broken down into three or five sub-moves, either two big advances and an intervening decline, which Elliott-wavers call an *ABC*, or three advances with two intervening declines, which is an *ABCDE*.

But what I could never understand is how an Elliott wave analyst could make a lengthy presentation detailing wave counts that told her that the market was about to do something and then say: But here is an equally detailed count that leads to the exact opposite conclusion.

Elliott wave counts seem to explain everything perfectly in hindsight, but they don't do nearly as well in real time. Long-term investors can live without them.

CHAPTER 10

CYCLES NOT BASED ON MARKET PRICES

There are several important non-price-based cycles that you should know about: the dividend-yield cycle, the debt cycle, and the interest-rate cycle. Most of them track one or more of the price-based cycles, but they have interesting characteristics of their own.

Dividend-Yield Cycle

Formerly, stock price cycles could be calculated using the *dividend yield*. The dividend yield for the Dow Jones Industrial Average (DJIA) used to fluctuate between 3 and 6 percent in round numbers. When stocks yielded 6 percent, you bought them; when they yielded 3 percent, you sold them. (This was the basis of the late, great Edson Gould's "Senti-Meter" indicator, which used to be a very accurate gauge of the relative valuations of stocks. See Figure 10-1.)

For those who now think that 6 percent is an unimaginable yield for stocks, remember that as recently as 1982 the dividend yield on the S&P 500 hit 6.7 percent.

Figure 10-1: Edson Gould's "Senti-Meter," Standard & Poor's 500 Index (S&P 500), 1870–Present.

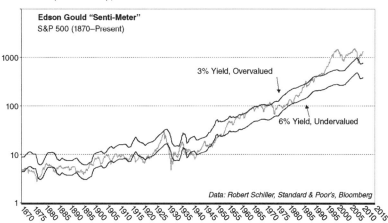

There are those who think that before the current secular valuation contraction is over, stock yields will approach 6 percent again. Yields tend to do this at secular market bottoms such as 1949, 1974, and 1982. In 1949, the yield was 6.5 percent.

Yields, of course, average less than 3 percent now, which causes great anxiety among investors, who think that stock prices must fall 50 percent to get back to a 6 percent yield. But, of course, this is not the only way dividends could approach 6 percent; companies also could start facing pressure to pay dividends from their shareholders again.

Historically, a much greater percentage of a corporation's income was paid in dividends than it is now. This changed because of the increased power of managements and the diminished power of stockholders. Stockholders used to have more of a say in management and used to demand dividends. Now management is tempted by stock options and absurd cash bonuses based on "reported" profitability. Well, let's face it, management is not correctly incented by these little goodies. Stock options give management an incentive to inflate stock prices and to use earnings for stock-repurchase programs, which inflate the value of their holdings. And management cash bonuses based on profitability encourage management to inflate current earnings, often at the expense of the company's long-term health and profitability.

In my opinion, at some point, managements are going to have to start sharing the wealth with their shareholders again. Instead of using excess money to buy back their own stock and attempt to push the stock price higher and inflate the value of their stock options, they're going to have to pay out bigger dividends to their shareholders.

The Debt Cycle

Several cycles lie outside the market but affect the market. The first is the debt cycle, which pretty much tracks the Kondratieff cycle.

If you chart the amount of debt outstanding per capita, you will find that it goes from a low number to a high number over a period of decades and decades, ultimately reaches a point of maximum extension, and then starts contracting. Household debt is now contracting. This is usually bad news for economic expansions because that's when you lose flexibility, lose the ability to make new investments, and lose your house.

It's not when things are good that investors make mistakes; it's when they project that things are going to continue to be good into the infinite future. This is when they get in trouble. Conversely, when things are bad, it's only when you project that they will continue to get bad into the infinite future that you get into trouble.

Bernard Baruch said it best: "I have always thought that if in the lamentable era of the new economics, culminating in 1929, even in the presence of the dizzily spiraling prices, we had all continuously repeated, 'Two and two still make four,' much of the evil might have been averted. Similarly, even in the general moment of gloom in which this Foreword was written [1932], where many were starting to wonder if declines would never halt, the abracadabra would be that they always did" (Bernard Baruch, from the Foreword to *Extraordinary Popular Delusions & the Madness of Crowds*, 1932).

The Interest-Rate Cycle

The *interest-rate cycle* correlates with the debt cycle. It is another long-term cycle.

Right now we are in a period where interest rates can't get much lower. Our short-term rates are effectively at zero, and our long-term rates are at about 3 percent.

If you really want to think scary thoughts, ask yourself what's going to happen when interest rates go back to more normal levels.

Short-term rates, for instance, affect our budget deficit. According to the ISI Group, right now we have something like $3 trillion in short-term debt, on which we are paying virtually no interest. More normal short-term rates are 3 to 3.5 percent and they reached about 20 percent not all that long ago. Each percentage increase in the interest rate will add $30 billion to our short-term borrowing costs.

Long-term interest rates are no less frightening. Now they hover between 3 and 4 percent. Within our investment life-times (in 1981), long-term interest rates also reached 20 per-cent. Well, 20 percent was not normal. But 3 and 4 percent long-term interest rates aren't normal either. So what happens when the pendulum swings back to a more normal interest rate?

This not only affects the budget deficit, but it also will have a huge impact on the economy and housing market. And, since bonds compete with stocks for a place in our investment port-folios, rising interest rates will, at some point, have a negative effect on stock prices as bonds become relatively attractive ver-sus stocks.

Other Cycles Not Based on Market Prices

One other non-market-based cycle deserves a brief mention since it is very much in the news as this goes to press thanks to the Occupy Wall Street movement: the income distribu-tion cycle. The share of pretax income received by the top 1 percent of Americans peaked at about 24 percent in 1928, fell to 9 percent in the early 1970s, and has now climbed back to the 1928 peak. Whatever you may think of the Occupy Wall Street movement, they do seem to have history on their side in that the "top 1%" percentage is much more likely to fall back to more "normal" levels over the long term than stay as high as it is now.

CHAPTER 11

TOPS AND BOTTOMS

In order to gain the right perspective, long-term investors should look at a weekly chart rather than a daily one. (I must confess, though, that when I first got into the business, I thought that weekly charts were glacially moving things with no action at all and paid absolutely no attention to them. It's a good thing for me that computer-generated intraday charts weren't available back then, and I had to confine my lust for constant action to daily charts. As I've matured, though, I've come to understand that for long-term investors, weekly charts are key.)

When you look at a stock chart—whether it's a daily, weekly, or monthly chart—you'll see one of four things:

1. *A top.* The stock is ending an advance and preparing to decline.
2. *A downtrend.* The stock is going down.
3. *A bottom.* The stock is ending a decline and is preparing to go up.
4. *An uptrend.* The stock is going up.

Of the four, tops and bottoms are by far the most important because they're signaling a change in trend rather than a continuation.

Tops

The first sign of a top is when the market or stock starts to lose momentum. There are all types of top formations—rounding tops, head-and-shoulders tops, ad infinitum—and discussing each one is beyond the scope of this book. (I'll take you through one, a head-and-shoulders top, in a minute to show you what a loss of momentum looks like on a chart; if you want to look at lots more top formations, my suggestions in the Appendix will point you in the right direction.)

Major market tops are likely to be slow, rounded things. The price is likely to stay fairly near the high for quite a while.

At the top, both the news and the economic outlook inevitably are good. But remember, the market will start to decline ahead of both the news and perceived changes to the economy.

When the market or a stock starts to move downward, it usually starts slowly.

The exception to this is when the top is a bubble top. In this case, the market is likely to be frothy and dangerous and reverse—when the time finally comes—very suddenly, generating large losses in a short period. Such tops are more rare than general market tops but are very, very dangerous when they happen.

The thing to remember about tops, though, is that they usually take a fair amount of time to form and are signaled by a visible loss of upside momentum and a gradual buildup of downside momentum. In addition, the news is inevitably good when it happens.

Head-and-Shoulders Tops

Near a top, nothing shows a loss of momentum quite like a head-and-shoulders top. Figure 11-1 shows an idealized head-and-shoulders top and demonstrates how a loss of upside momentum shows up on a chart. The wave consists of six elements:

1. An initial rally to what will become the *left shoulder*
2. An initial decline to what will become the *neckline*
3. A second rally to a higher high that will become the *head* (Note, though, that at this point the stock still

Figure 11-1: Head-and-Shoulders Top.

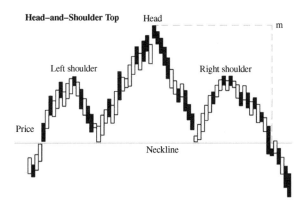

Source: Wikipedia

145

looks fine; the second rally carried it to a significantly higher high and was much bigger than the initial decline. At this point, then, the stock hasn't lost any momentum yet.)

4. A second decline that retraces the entire preceding rally and carries the stock back to the *neckline* (This is the first sign that the stock has started to lose upside momentum; the second decline, unlike the first, was as big as the prior advance—and the second decline was much bigger than the initial decline. A caution flag is now waving.)

5. A third rally that does not take the stock to a new high but only back to a *right shoulder* (This is where the situation starts to get really serious; the third rally was significantly less than the second one, and even worse, it didn't retrace all the prior decline. This means that a serious loss of upside momentum now has occurred.)

6. A final decline that breaks the two prior lows—the *neckline*—and completes the *head-and-shoulders top*

The main lesson from the chart of a head-and-shoulders top is not that the stock has made a classic top but that it had a significant move but now has lost significant upside momentum and is starting to build downside momentum. And this is a precondition for a downside reversal.

If you are lucky, you can figure out how quickly the stock is losing momentum so that you can stick with it as long as you can. Remember that stocks go up the fastest at the beginning of a bull market and then gradually go up less and less fast— but they still keep going up. This means that once the stock has had its initial rally, it will be losing momentum all the way to the top. What you need to know, then, is when that loss of momentum starts getting serious. Thus, if you have a rally of 10 percent, and the next rally is 8 percent, and the next rally is 6 percent, and the next rally is 4 percent, as long as the declines aren't getting terribly more serious and the stock is still going higher, you are right to keep holding the stock. Ideally, you would go up 10 percent and down 4 percent, up 8 percent and down 5 percent, up 6 percent and down 6 percent, and then up 4 percent and down 6 percent. So you are gradually losing that upward progression, but it can take a good long time to do so. If you're looking at a weekly chart, in fact, the process can take several years to play out.

Anecdote—Nothing as Bullish as a Failed Head-and-Shoulders Top

The late Mike Epstein, who was a trader at Cowen & Co. for decades, was one of the smartest people I've ever known. He could impart more wisdom in one sentence than most people could in a couple of paragraphs.

One day, while I was participating in an American Association of Professional Technical Analysts brainstorming session, Mike casually remarked, "There's nothing as bullish as a failed head-and-shoulders top."

Just that.

What he meant was that the stock had gone through every single step of making a top: It lost momentum, it broke through a series of lows, it had everything going against it, but then it failed to go down and instead went back up. It was just like in the Rocky movies. Investors hit that stock with everything they had—everything—and it still managed to get up off the floor.

And that's a failed head-and-shoulders top.

That stock could be a "buy."

You also need to put the stock chart into a broader context. Where is the broad market? And then, where is the sector?

The Nasdaq peaked in April 2000 after rising for years. The very last stock I would want to buy would be a technology stock breaking out of a big base in February 2000. It's too late. The stock could have the most classic chart pattern in the universe, worthy of inclusion in any chart textbook ever published. But if it took the stock all the way until February 2000 to get going, after similar stocks had been going up for years and years, then something is wrong.

You can never just say that a stock breaking out of a base pattern is always bullish. Maybe not. Similarly, a stock breaking down from a top pattern is not always bearish.

You have to put everything in context.

Bottoms

Major bottoms are scary things. There is a dearth of rationality, and volatility is very high. Some bottoms show rounded patterns, but most are much more erratic than that. The market lurches and dives.

Remember, fear is a much stronger emotion than greed. Market bottoms usually are much more volatile than market tops, and they affect everyone in the market. Yes, there are panicked sales by unsophisticated investors, but that is only the tip of the iceberg.

Institutional investors may have sold already because they anticipate bad news. Then the market goes down, then the news explains why the market is going down, and then individual investors also sell. In essence, in bear markets, where everyone is on edge and nervous, the news may affect the market just by creating emotion.

Fund managers whose funds are under water will be under pressure to "do something"—anything—to prevent further loss. So their trading can be a factor. Programmed trading may kick in and sell individual stocks using parameters that are designed to recognize companies in trouble and not a whole market in decline.

Speculators and short-term traders, of course, also sell into declining markets. They expect to be able to pick up the stocks cheaper later on.

But what really causes instability right near the bottom is forced selling.

Let's say that Mr. Hedge Fund Manager buys four times as much stock as he has money. For every $25 he has, he has bought $100 of stocks by using $25 of the hedge fund's money and borrowing $75 of the broker's money.

Should the stock go down 20 percent, which is very easy for a volatile stock to do in a bear market, the lender now has lent $75 on what is now an $80 stock. A $5 cushion is not what the lender bargained for. So she calls the hedge fund and asks for more money. If the hedge fund has the money, all is well and good, but if it hasn't, the lender sells out the position, takes her $75, and gives the hedge fund whatever's left. And by that time, it's probably only $1 or $2.

The most ruthless sellers Wall Street has ever known are margin clerks. These clerks protect their firms' investments, their firms' loans. They don't care what they sell the stock for, so long as they get their $75 back. The result? You often get large blocks of stock subject to forced selling after the market has already gone down—a lot.

So every day when the market goes down, margin clerks calculate how much equity is left in the account, meaning how much of the margin buyer's skin is still in the game and how much has been sandpapered away. And if the stockholder doesn't have enough skin left, the margin clerk sends out a note demanding more money—a *margin call*. The calls go out twice a day. If the borrower meets the margin call, all is well and good. If the borrower does not meet the margin call, the stock is sold—immediately.

And the hedge fund? The net result—a $1 return on its $25 investment—has been a 96 percent loss. And this can spark other adjustments by the hedge fund, other selling.

So very often, those horrific down days are not created by simple, plain-vanilla panic selling, although admittedly this plays a role. The really violent selling pressure comes from margin calls not being met and the subsequent margin selling. Forced margin selling will be highest at the bottom. Once that borrowed money and those highly leveraged positions have been flushed out, you have reached a bottom.

In 2008, the real estate bubble ended up in the same way. Many highly engineered financial instruments were created out of pools of real estate loans, and these highly engineered things were bought with a lot of borrowed money. When the real estate market crashed, it led to forced selling of those highly engineered instruments and a bottom in real estate instruments.

Anecdote—Forced Selling on a Grand Scale

In 1974, the stock market had gone down during the prior year or so, from 1,000 to the mid-600s. New York State authorities then went to a certain insurance company and said, "You are not meeting your statutory reserve requirements. You have to raise money to meet those requirements." The only way the insurance company could do that was to sell stocks; the company was forced by the authorities to sell a lot of stock into a nervous and illiquid market where prices had already gone down for a very long time and historically were very, very low.

And so the last leg of that bear market, the leg that sent prices down to the 1974 low, was generated by an insurance company that became affectionately known on Wall Street as the "Mad Bomber." This company almost single-handedly sent the Dow Jones Industrials down from 680 on September 24 to 573 on October 3, 1974, via its selling and the margin calls that went out as a result.

151

> It wasn't because the insurance company wanted to sell—it was because it was forced to sell. (Of course, the same thing is happening in real estate now—forced sales into down markets.)

Head-and-Shoulders Bottoms

Head-and-shoulders bottoms also happen. They are called *inverse head and shoulders* and show a loss of momentum on the downside.

To get an idea of what one looks like, go back to Figure 11-1, showing the head-and-shoulders top, and turn the book upside down.

The stock goes down and makes a low. The stock rallies. The stock goes down again and makes a lower low. The stock rallies. The stock goes down again, but not so low. Then it rallies again and finally goes up through the neckline.

You've lost momentum, but this time you've lost downside momentum.

Rocky's getting ready to get up off the floor.

Flags and Other Patterns

There are zillions of other patterns. I try to stay away from patterns because they tend to force things into a mold. Sometimes patterns work; sometimes they don't.

The important thing is what the patterns are trying to measure. For instance, normally, when a stock runs up 10 percent, it takes a rest and makes some sort of what is called a *consolidation pattern*. What precise form that consolidation pattern—a flag, a pennant, an ascending triangle, and so on—isn't really important. The important thing is that the stock has rallied a significant amount, rests for a while, and then is ready to start back up again. If you want to force that consolidation into a pattern, and if you want to call that pattern a flag, or a pennant, or whatever, fine, but the best thing to do is to say it's consolidating, whatever form that consolidation takes.

Quite a few patterns are denoted by technical jargon that means absolutely nothing to the average investor or the average portfolio manager. You can convey a point and communicate effectively without using jargon—jargon only confuses things. (This is another thing Bob Farrell has taught me and which all too few fellow technicians have learned. KISS—Keep it simple, stupid!)

Usually the head-and-shoulders top or bottom is such an obvious pattern that I describe it as such. But other than that, I just say that the stock has completed a bottom and is now rallying. It is in a phase of its advance, and then it consolidates. Ultimately, it begins another leg on the upside. And then it loses momentum and goes through some sort of topping process, completes it, goes down, has multiple legs on the downside, and finally goes into some sort of bottoming process.

Saying *bottoming process* is a whole lot better than trying to force one of 18 gibberishy-sounding bottoming pattern labels on it.

PART V

INDICATORS

CHAPTER 12

TREND INDICATORS

An indicator can be anything that forecasts a change in stock prices—anything at all as long as it is reliable and works consistently.

Indicators come in all shapes and sizes. Some garner attention through a combination of coincident accuracy and silliness. For a while, women's skirt lengths appeared to rise and fall with the markets. (During periods of shortening hemlines, technicians got a great deal of amusement drawing trend lines on pictures illustrating the phenomenon.) A Super Bowl victory by an NFC team predicted an up market (a way-up market for a Steelers victory, says Susan), and an AFC victory led to a down market.

Philip Maymim of New York University has even developed a musical indicator. According to this, market volatility correlates inversely with the complexity of song beats. (The rationale is that during difficult times, market participants prefer a simple, comforting beat, and vice versa.) But since the traders must be nervous already when they select their calming playlists, I'd rather use this indicator to predict trends in music, not to buy stocks.

A savvy technical investor always has certain broad indicators in his back pocket, ready to review at a moment's notice. He knows where the market is within the Kondratieff and four-year cycles. He knows where in the interest-rate and dividend-yield cycles he is. He knows where the last major bottoms and tops are. He knows whether current market sentiment is extremely optimistic or pessimistic. He knows what the current chart pattern looks like.

And that's what he starts with.

He's ready for the next move. He's ready to use other indicators as guideposts. But which ones?

Indicators

Indicators can give confirmatory or contradictory advice. A *confirming indicator* is one that says, "John Smith says cotton prices are going to rise, and Smith is always right." A *contradictory indicator* says, "John Smith says cotton prices are going to fall, and Smith is always wrong." Either of these can be valid indicators that the price of cotton is going to rise. (*Note*: Contradictory indicators should not be confused with contrary indicators, which are described below.)

In addition, there are two main types of indicators: *trend indicators* and *contrary indicators* (or indicators that lean one way or the other). This simply means that the indicators either have a bias toward recognizing continuity (trend) or recognizing potential change (contrary).

Each approach has a weaknesses: A trend indicator may be late to show a change in the current trend, whereas a contrary indicator may be early. Investors have to ask themselves which they want to be (on average)—late or early. For most small investors, trend indicators work better and are a lower-risk proposition. For large institutional money managers, contrary indicators are the only way to go because once they decide to buy, they buy in sizes large enough to move the market. (An exception may be during turbulent bottoms, where the sheer amount of panicked and forced selling can hide large purchases.)

Even the best indicators, though, are never infallible; they dictate probability, not certainty. (As legendary analyst Stan Berge from Tucker Anthony and R. L. Day always reminded us, "Remember that we are dealing with probabilities, not certainties.") If an indicator says that a stock price should go up, in 77 percent of cases the stock may go up, but in 23 percent the stock may go down. No indicator works all the time. And even working indicators usually can't predict bottoms and tops precisely.

So pick your poison, and remember Bernard Baruch's famous quote: "Don't try to buy at the bottom and sell at the top. This can't be done, except by liars."

Remember, News Is Not an Indicator, Primary or Otherwise

This bears repeating.

All too many investors stick to the one indicator that doesn't work—the news. It's hard for investors to accept this. They do not track their investments regularly and are more likely to do so when the economy makes the headlines. At these points, the news is likely to be very consistent—either all good or all bad. But it's also very, very likely to have been discounted already by the market.

As Bob Farrell puts it, "The market anticipates, while the news exaggerates."

News may affect the markets only in the very late stages of a bull or bear market, where omnipresent good news or bad news sparks a late round of panic buying or selling by unsophisticated investors.

Trend Analysis—Don't Fight the Tape

The most basic trend indicator for the market, of course, is the direction prices are currently going. Wall Street even has a saying for respecting the trend: "Don't fight the tape." If the current trend is up, expect it to continue in the same direction. If the current trend is down, ditto.

If the market is in an uptrend, it's going up. It makes no sense to insist that the market is "too high" or "overbought" and therefore has to go down. This may be a time to watch the market carefully but not necessarily a time to sell.

An overbought market may reverse, and you may see it coming, but don't insist that it's going to reverse before it actually starts doing so.

And remember that trends you're concerned with last weeks and months, not hours or days.

The trend is your friend. And being a little late to recognize it isn't nearly as bad as ignoring it altogether.

There are many trend indicators that make recognizing a current trend easier by smoothing out daily gyrations in the stock price. Most are available in the standard charting packages on the Internet.

Trend channels are useful to view the direction of the current trend. Most technicians create them by drawing straight lines that connect highs to highs and lows to lows. The charting packages also have a number of indicators that draw envelopes around the stock's price that are some specific distance away from it. As long as the stock is trading within that channel or that envelope, it's moving within the trend.

Cycle Analysis and the Underlying Trend—
Frank Peluso

Trends are never static. Prices may be moving in one direction, in a general way, but the force behind the trend is always changing. *Cycle analysis* can supplement trend analysis by helping to identify changes in the underlying trend.

Frank Peluso was an extremely gifted technical analyst who worked at Jesup and Lamont while I was at the Manhattan Fund and then at Putnam. Frank taught me more about cycles than anyone else; his background was in physics, and he likened cycle analysis to the swing of a pendulum. The price starts down, it accelerates, it reaches its maximum point of acceleration, it then decelerates, and finally, it ends at an extreme on the other side.

So the concept of cycle analysis is this: Where is the pendulum in its arc? Is it going up or down? Accelerating or decelerating?

The most interesting thing about cycle analysis, though, is what happens when it is wrong.

Frank called this the concept of the *underlying trend*. It was one of the most important things I ever learned.

Anecdote—The Importance of the Underlying Trend

Frank had come to the Manhattan Fund to introduce himself. In those days, he broke the market down into 2- to 10-day cycles, 2- to 10-week cycles, and 2- to 10-month cycles. He offered to share his buy and sell signals with us for a while to let us evaluate them, and Gerry Tsai, who ran the fund, was receptive.

Shortly afterward, I got a call. "We just got a 2- to 10-day buy signal."

Gerry, who was bullish in a falling market, was very pleased.

Fewer than two days later, I got another call. "We just got a 2- to 10-day sell signal."

Gerry was furious; the market had been going against him, he was looking for some respite, and "It didn't even go up for two days!" As far as Gerry was concerned, that was the end of Frank Peluso.

I reported this to Frank, who quickly told me, "No, Walter; you don't understand. When a cycle doesn't meet its normal expectations, it means the next higher cycle is unusually powerful. The underlying trend is unusually strong."

> And so it was; following the aborted 2- to 10-day buy signal, the market went down—hard—for the next nine days.

The lesson here is that if the market "should" do something but doesn't, it's an indication that the next-longer trend is unusually powerful—powerful enough to prevent the market from doing what it "should" do—and that powerful underlying trend is probably going to make itself felt on the next move. And this can be an invaluable piece of information to a technically savvy investor.

Breadth Indicators

While trend indicators show the direction of the market, *breadth indicators* show how healthy the move is. A broadly based advance, one that involves nearly every stock in the market, is likely to last a long time. An advance that depends on a few sectors will peter out faster. An advance that depends on just one sector or just a few leading stocks already may have evolved into a bear market.

The *advance-decline line* tells you how many issues have gone up compared with how many issues have gone down and therefore how broadly based the advance is. It's calculated simply by taking the number of advancing stocks each day, subtracting the number of declining stocks, and adding that to the previous day's number. (You can start with any number you want; it's the advance-decline line relative to itself that's important, not a specific level.) To signal the end of a broad bull market, look for a peak in the advance-decline line.

At the beginning of a bull market, money flows into the market on such a broad front and on such a large scale that everything goes up. And then, after a while, the amount of money coming in diminishes, and most stocks go up. Then, after a while longer, the amount of money diminishes still further, and then just some stocks go up. Toward the end, the amount of money coming into the market is so small that only a few stocks go up. The advance-decline line will reflect all this.

Another way to look at breadth is to measure the number of industry groups that are trading above some trend-defining moving average. That number will be 100 percent at the beginning of a bull market and decline gradually as the bull market matures.

The concept of breadth also works for sectors within the market. If technology as a whole, for example, has more decliners than advancers, it may signal that the sector has reached a top despite a rising price and a continued (but lower) flow of money into it. All that money may be going into one huge company, such as Apple.

Speculative Activity Analysis

Speculative activity indicators show the level of speculative trading compared with the volume in more conservative stocks. The most basic way to do that today is to compare

Nasdaq volume with New York Stock Exchange (NYSE) volume.

Tony Tabell, one of my great technical mentors who was at Walston when I first met him and subsequently branched out on his own, did it like this: He took the basic ratio comparing the volume on the American Stock Exchange (AMEX) with the volume on the NYSE (there was no Nasdaq volume back then, and there actually was some volume on the AMEX to measure), then normalized it by calculating a 4-week moving average of the ratio and a 52-week moving average of the ratio, and finally compared the short-term (4-week) moving average with the long-term (52-week) moving average. In this way, he got a ratio that oscillated around 1.00 (when the 4- and 52-week averages were the same).

Today, of course, we use Nasdaq volume rather than AMEX. If the ratio gets up to 1.18, it's a warning that speculative activity is too high. And if it gets up above 1.27, it's a sign of clear and present danger.

Normalizing the data removes the long-term bias caused by such things as the fact that volume on the NYSE is in a long-term downtrend because trading is moving off the floor. As these long-term changes take place, they are automatically incorporated into the 4- and 52-week moving averages.

In the old days, we also tracked margin buying to determine excessive speculative activity. Now, though, there are so many other ways to leverage positions that margin debt has fallen by the wayside as a measurement. To leverage, you can buy things such as a Standard & Poor's 500 Index (S&P 500) exchange-traded fund (ETF) that moves up and down twice as

fast—or even three times as fast—as the S&P 500. You can buy
S&P futures, you can buy options, and you can do all sorts of
things. You can do all sorts of leveraging without having to go
on margin. If someone thinks that New Hampshire Pharma-
ceuticals has a new drug that is going to go wild, she'll go out
and buy options on it rather than buy the stock on margin. It's
more leverage, it's cheaper, it's the quickest way to get bang for
the buck—and it's also the quickest way to lose all your money
if you're wrong.

Many analysts use option trading data to measure speculative activity. But option trading may be coming from people
who are usually right, such as hedge fund managers, or people
who are usually wrong, and the trick is to find out which is
which. I'm still working on this.

Anecdote—Speculation on the AMEX

During the go-go years of the late 1960s, volume on the
AMEX reached as much as 60 or 70 percent of the volume
on the NYSE. And for two days in May 1961, AMEX volume actually exceeded that of the NYSE, thanks to some
very low-priced stocks such as Sapphire Petroleum and
Israel-American Oil.

The exceptionally heavy volume in the speculative stocks
on the AMEX was a pretty darn good sign that speculative
enthusiasm was at an unsustainably high level—and it ultimately led to the crash of 1962.

Exception Analysis—John Bennett

I was first introduced to the concept of exception analysis by John Bennett, whose promotion from head of Putnam's Market Analysis Department to Director of Research in 1970 created the opening that I filled. *Exception analysis* is the idea of following many indicators, which most market analysts do today but didn't do back then. When the indicators are within normal bounds, we simply ignore them. (As John Bollinger, of Bollinger Band fame, once astutely remarked, "No indicator speaks all the time.") But when the indicators exceed normal bounds in one direction or the other, we pay attention. Some indicators send messages only every couple of years, but when they send a message, it can be an extremely important one.

This can be particularly useful with indicators that show the amount of speculation. Most of the time, speculative activity in the market remains within normal bounds, but every once in a while it gets dangerously high, and it is then that you take the indicator's message into account and draw a conclusion from it. In this case, of course, the conclusion would be that the market is making an important top.

Relative Strength

If you are following a piece of the market, such as an individual stock or sector, you also should track what that stock is doing relative to a larger related group.

So compare the stock to a sector, a sector to an index, and an index to the broad market. Is it stronger or weaker than the larger group?

The leadership in a new bull market telegraphs its intentions by generating relative strength toward the end of the prior bear market.

Relative strength is an extremely important subject. I'll discuss it more fully in Chapter 13 (Market Sectors as Indicators) and Chapter 16 (Selecting Individual Stocks).

A Promising New Indicator

One indicator that I have high hopes for is from the International Securities Exchange, which is one of the largest options exchanges in the world. This exchange calculates something it calls the *ISEE index*, which is a call-put ratio that measures only "opening buy" transactions by the public. (*Public* is described as a noninstitutional and non–brokerage house investor, and an *opening buy* is an initial transaction.)

Say that you are sitting at your computer and you suddenly decide that the market is going up. You rush in and buy some Apple call options. This is an opening-buy transaction; you're buying options that you didn't own before. Let's say that you buy 100 call options. So the opening-buy call volume is now 100. Okay? When you sell the options, call volume is going to be 100 again. But it's not an opening buy because you are selling and closing your position. It's a *closing sale*. So it doesn't show up in the opening-buy data.

So what the ISEE ratio does is measure new buying activity in both call options (which, of course, are vehicles where you think the price is going to go up) and put options (where you think the price is going to go down).

I still have hopes that this is going to be a valuable indicator, but I'm still trying to figure out whether bursts of activity reflect "usually right" or "usually wrong" players and thus represent a contrary signal or not. For example, in the middle of December 2010, the call-put ratio rose to near-record levels for a week or so. I interpreted that as a signal that everybody was positioning themselves for the traditional year-end rally and therefore that the year-end rally may have taken place already. But, as it turned out, all those people who bought all those calls were right because the market worked its way higher by the end of the year. More recently, though, the ISEE ratio proved its value by reflecting an orgy of put buying every time the S&P got below 1125 in August and September of 2011; it traded 100 points higher shortly afterward.

Again, I don't care whether a group of investors is always right or always wrong—as long as they are consistent. And I'm not sure yet whether the ISEE call-put ratio is a consistently contrary signal or not.

Anecdote—A Historic Indicator

Back in the 1960s, a lot of market activity was done in odd lots, that is, lots of less than 100 shares. And we got some great indicators from the odd-lot trading data.

Why were odd lots so important?

At the time, purchasing a round lot of stock (that is, 100 shares) for, say, $4,000 was out of the range of most salaried people. (In 1959, the average annual income was only

$5,000, the price of a new car was $2,200, and the average price of a house was $30,000.)

In order to encourage people to invest in stocks, the NYSE and Merrill Lynch came up with something called the "Monthly Investment Plan," which let small investors buy as little as just $40 of a stock every month. The advertising campaigns urged people to "Own Your Share of American Business." The concept was called "People's Capitalism."

The average price of a stock in those days was about $40, so you needed $4,000 to buy a round lot. On a $40 monthly accumulation plan, then, it would take you 100 months to build up enough to buy 100 shares. So odd lots were very, very actively traded back then as a way for people to buy stock in less than carload lots. In the 1950s, in fact, odd-lot volume was roughly 10 percent of round-lot volume on the NYSE.

There were only two odd-lot brokers. Merrill Lynch, being the fair and benevolent behemoth that it was, did its odd-lot business with one of the brokers for a couple of months and then did business with the other one for a couple of months. So we were able to get detailed odd-lot numbers from both brokers.

In those days, as I said, odd lots comprised about 10 percent of NYSE volume. It was really big. And it was a wonderful sample because each one of these millions of shares of activity was in blocks of less than 100 shares. The data therefore reflected what a lot of people were doing.

This gave us a great sentiment indicator that measured what mass psychology was.

At Merrill Lynch, we got odd-lot trading broken down into purchases and sales and short sales, along with everybody else, but we also got the changes in the odd-lot houses' inventories. Those two brokerage houses were among the most intelligent Wall Street traders ever in terms of managing their inventories—which they did constantly. When an odd-lot house got an order to sell 50 shares of IBM, for example, it had to buy 100 shares of the stock on the NYSE to be able to sell 50 shares to its customer. It then could do one of two things: either keep the remaining 50 shares in inventory or sell 100 shares on the floor and be short 50 shares. How the brokers managed their inventories, whether they were in a net long or a net short position, was a terrific indicator of what the stock market was going to do.

Unfortunately, odd-lot trading has gone the way of the dodo and is now just another example of the many indicators that used to work really, really well but no longer exist.

CHAPTER **13**

MARKET SECTORS AS INDICATORS

Introduction to Sector Funds

If you are following a piece of the market, you need to track what that piece is doing relative to a larger related group—its relative strength—as well as its price. So compare a stock with a group, a group with a sector, and a sector with the broad market. Is it stronger or weaker than the larger group?

In this sort of analysis, market sectors play a critical role. But because this is an evolving area, some background information is needed to understand where sectors came from and where they are headed.

The first sector work was done in the early 1960s by Ken Safian and the late Ken Smilen, then at Purcell Graham, who came up with what they called the *dual-market principle*. They were the first to break the market down beyond the market itself, and they broke it down into two sectors—growth and cyclical.

They found (not surprisingly) that the growth sector performed much differently than the cyclical sector. They therefore followed and successfully forecast two stock markets rather than one. Later, Standard & Poor's (S&P) came along and broke the S&P 500 Index into nine market sectors, which is basically what we use today.

Wall Street also created a number of investment vehicles to enable people to invest in specific market sectors. Tracking activity in those vehicles provided us with some terrific insights—for a while.

In the 1980s, Fidelity introduced sector funds, and for a while, movements in and out of these funds provided one of the most reliable market indicators around.

Fidelity's sector funds were designed for active traders, so they were priced every hour rather than just once a day. At the time, Fidelity charged 2 percent to buy one of the funds and another 1 percent to redeem it. A Fidelity fund manager (who has long since retired) described them to me as "a big casino."

"We have a lot of sector funds," he explained. "So we have a lot of games for people to play. We charge them 2 percent to come into the casino and another 1 percent to leave the casino—and we don't care what they do while they are in there."

So sector fund investors who wanted to move to the sidelines for a while tended to leave their money in the casino because of the entry and exit fees. To accommodate them, Fidelity set up a select money-market fund where they could "park" their inactive money within the casino.

These Fidelity sector funds were huge. At one point, they contained $20 billion of assets. There were lots of investors with a wide range of interests and skill levels. And any money that wasn't involved directly in sector fund investing usually was in the select money-market fund.

Fidelity released, on a daily basis, the assets in each of its sector funds. So I could take the ratio of the amount of money in the select money-market fund and compare it with the amount of money in the sector funds as a whole. It was an absolutely splendid measure of what the aggressive investing public was doing in the stock market!

Like all indicators of this type, it was a contrary indicator. The amount of cash was very low at market highs and very high at market lows.

It worked wonderfully for many, many years—until it didn't. First, the Securities and Exchange Commission (SEC) disallowed redemption fees, so people were no longer forced to stay in the sector group of funds when they went to the sidelines. Second, the select money-market fund was paying a bit more than other Fidelity money-market funds, and it quickly attracted a huge amount of money from non–sector fund players; the percentage of sector fund assets in the money-market account, which had been swinging from roughly 3 percent to roughly 8 percent, ballooned to 25 percent.

Fidelity then decided to price the sector funds only once a day and placed restrictions on the amount of trading their clients could do in them in order to make them more of an investment vehicle than they had been previously.

The bottom line: Aggressive sector fund investors moved to exchange traded funds (EFTs), the select money-market fund attracted non–sector fund traders, and the daily data were discontinued, all of which rendered the indicator useless. But the information was great while it lasted, and is still instructive as to how that type of indicator can work.

Before moving on, I should note that Fidelity's 39 sector funds still give me some very valuable insights. Just after they were first launched, Dean LeBaron casually remarked to me, "I think there's some information there." What he meant was that Fidelity's sector funds were actively managed portfolios, not the passively managed groups that we had all been analyzing up until then. I started doing relative strength work on Fidelity's sector funds as a result, which meant I was comparing the best-perceived technology stocks with the best-perceived energy stocks, the best-perceived financial stocks, and so on, and this has indeed generated much better results than relative strength work on passively managed groups.

Fortunately, I found a replacement for the now-sidelined Fidelity sector fund cash/asset ratio. The Rydex group of funds offered a group of index funds, some of which moved in line with the indexes themselves, some of which moved inversely with the indexes themselves, and some of which moved twice as fast as the indexes themselves. And Rydex allowed—even encouraged—investors to move among the funds, which were priced twice daily. The assets in each of the Rydex funds were updated every night, a little after midnight. By getting up very early in the morning, I could get the previous day's data and could see whether money flowed into or out of the bullish funds that moved in line with the indexes and whether money moved into or out of the inverse funds that moved in the opposite direction of the index funds. (If the S&P goes down 1 percent, the S&P inverse fund goes up 1 percent.) So, if you think the market is going down, you want to own an inverse fund. It's a way to sell short without actually being short. It's a way to either hedge against positions you already own or actually to bet on a market decline.

And it's not a notional bet. You are buying a fund that is actually short the underlying securities. Either the fund is short something like S&P futures contracts or it owns something like swaps—but it is actually short the index or the component stocks, usually through derivatives; it's not just a notional bet. If Rydex investors sell $300 million of the S&P 500 fund, there will be $300 million worth of the S&P 500 sold in some way, shape, or form in the market.

The thing I looked for, though, was not how trading in the Rydex funds affected the market—it was the sentiment. Were people buying or selling? Did they consider a decline in the stock market a buying opportunity, or were they fearful and running for the exits? If they considered it a buying opportunity, the market usually continued to go down until they got scared. And this has been true ever since the days when I tracked the market through Merrill Lynch margin accounts for Bob Farrell—investors tended to buy early into declines and sell late into declines.

They also would tend to be cautious in the early stages of an advance and then get enthusiastic in the later stages. And remember, these trades involved real money. I was not looking at a survey of investor opinion; I was measuring actual transactions with real dollars in the marketplace. As always, I was watching their feet, not their mouths.

I mentioned that the Rydex funds were priced twice a day. Unfortunately, ETFs came along, and they were priced continuously. So gradually they lured more and more assets away from the Rydex funds, and the Rydex fund activity became dominated by relatively few market timers rather than reflecting what a broad population was doing. From an analytical standpoint, it's not helpful to measure what a small population is doing. So the investment activity reflected in the Rydex funds became less and less representative. And gradually, it faded away in significance.

Again, as with any sentiment indicator, you want to follow a group of investors who are either always right or always wrong. It matters not which they are—as long as they are consistent. And the problem with the Rydex funds was that as the number of people participating shrunk, their track record became better. And so, instead of being a consistently contrary indicator, it turned into an indicator that often was contrary— but also often right because you're not going to survive as an investor managing large sums of money in vehicles such as this unless you are right more often than not. So all of a sudden the contrary part of the indicator also faded. But, again, the information was great while it lasted, and is still instructive as to how that type of indicator can work.

When I had to stop relying on the Rydex data, I started tracking the money inflows and outflows in the ETFs that tracked the S&P 500 and the Nasdaq. Here, again, there were ETFs that reflected the index itself and moved in line with the index. There also were ETFs that moved inversely with the index. And there were ETFs that moved in line or inversely with the index but twice as fast. I tracked the money flows in all of them.

So, for example, let's say that the S&P 500 ETF has $100 million in assets and the S&P 500 goes up 1 percent. This means that there should be $101 million in the ETF that night. If there is more than that, it means that money has come into the ETF. If there is less than that, it means that money has gone out. So all you need to know is the amount of assets in each ETF every day and the percentage move of each ETF every day, and you can calculate the amount of money that flows into or out of each ETF each day.

The problem is that everybody from major hedge funds to the general public uses these ETFs, so when you get a big surge of money coming in an index ETF, it's impossible to tell whether it is smart money or dumb money—whether it is the most sophisticated, most profitable hedge fund starting to buy or the public rushing in to buy. So I gave up following them because I couldn't reliably differentiate between money flows that indicated that something was going to happen and money flows that indicated to go contrary. In other words, I couldn't tell whether ETF money flows were a confirming indicator or a contrary indicator. They ended up being a little bit of both.

So three of my favorite sentiment indicators have gone by the wayside. But there still is lots of good investment information to be mined from the sector funds.

Using Sector Funds

It used to be that if you were buying the market, you would buy something that tracked the S&P 500 and move in and out of it. But with sector funds, you can be more precise. For example, if you think everything in the market looks good

179

except for financial stocks, you can buy all the sectors except financials. And now you own the S&P 500 minus financials. If the only stocks that you think are worthy of investing in are the cyclically exposed materials and industrials sectors, you can just buy those two ETFs. You also can have a double position in your favorite sector and a less-than-average weighting in your least-favorite sector.

Although you can be more flexible in your investing, you also now need to have nine market opinions to back up your decisions. For example, during the energy boom of the 1980s, the energy sector performed very well, and you had to analyze energy, and then you had to analyze the rest of the market. In 1999 and early 2000, the technology sector was *the* place to be, and you could ignore the other eight sectors of the market and just stay in technology. And then technology had a great bear market, and the rest of the market did very well. So you had to analyze technology as well as the rest of the market.

When I say, "The market is bullish"—when I make a market judgment—I'm trying to predict the S&P 500, which is the benchmark that institutions use. But if the S&P 500 goes up 5 percent, that doesn't necessarily mean that the financial sector is going up 5 percent, or that technology stocks are going up 5 percent, or that energy stocks are going up 5 percent. So the next order of business is to determine which sectors are likely to do better and which sectors are at risk of doing worse. Everything used to move together, and you could issue a single market opinion. If the market went up, just about everything went up. These days, there is so much sector differentiation that you really need to go beyond the one-word market description.

The nine major sectors today are as follows:

1. Consumer discretionary
2. Consumer staples
3. Energy
4. Financials
5. Health care
6. Industrials
7. Materials
8. Technology
9. Utilities

Leading Indicators Generally

In general, sectors follow a pattern. Financials traditionally are the first sector in the market to move up or down, and the energy sector traditionally is the last to move.

Some sectors are more volatile than others. The materials sector, which is metal and lumber and so on, traditionally is more volatile than the other sectors. But when technology was leading the advance in 1999, it went up faster than anything. And when technology was not leading in the middle of the last decade, it didn't go up as fast as it used to.

The consumer-oriented sectors—consumer discretionary and consumer staples—traditionally are less volatile.

The Changing Role of Financials

It's hard to believe now, but back in the 1960s and 1970s, financial stocks were not a major factor in the stock market.

Almost all of them were traded over the counter. This was before the Nasdaq came into being, and over-the-counter (OTC) stocks were traded by market makers setting a bid price and then adding a markup, and that was the offering price. The difference was more than 7 percent in most cases. (I checked a quote for Bankers Trust in a 1962 *Wall Street Journal*: 51½ bid and 56 asked!) Not surprisingly, the OTC market was not nearly as active back then as it became after the Nasdaq system came into being. Also, in those days, banks were managed as banks used to be managed—very conservatively—so they were not volatile at all and usually were considered too dull to be interesting investments other than for people seeking stability and conservative dividend yields. Banks were considered to be a lot more like utilities than like aggressive stocks.

It wasn't until the bankers learned about leverage, stock options, and bonuses that banking stocks became more and more volatile.

Also, there were no publicly traded brokerage stocks in the 1960s. Donaldson, Lufkin & Jenrette was the first to go public, in 1970, and Merrill Lynch soon followed. But there were no publicly traded brokerage stocks before then and still only a few in the 1970s.

Financial stocks, though, ultimately became the biggest part of the S&P 500 Index.

But here's the problem with that. Financial companies don't really create anything. There is no production. If you create a bunch of mortgages, then slice them and dice them, and repackage them and sell them, you haven't really fulfilled an economic need. You haven't created jobs or anything. So an awful lot of what goes on in the financial sector is nothing more than financial engineering, which doesn't really add any-thing to the net economy.

Every once in a while, just to reassure myself that Amer-ica still makes things, I go up to Folkston, Georgia, where the tracks for the CSX trains coming down the East Coast and the tracks for the trains coming down from the Midwest merge together for 20 miles as they go around the Okefenokee Swamp. The area is well known to rail fans as the "Folkston Funnel," and 60 to 70 freight trains go through it every day. I go up to watch them. I find it refreshing to see that there is still some real production going on in America. I'm able to see chemical cars, raw materials cars, auto carriers, and cars with truck trailers—all sorts of things from the real economy.

But the financial stuff is just slicing and dicing. Some-body merges with somebody—that doesn't do anything, really. All that happens is they lay off a bunch of people. They say efficiencies are gained. But are they?

Based on current trends, in fact, there is a very good chance that the financial sector will lose its position of prominence in the S&P 500 in the coming years.

Lagging Indicators Generally

Energy and energy production companies traditionally lag behind the overall market. This has not changed despite per-ceived risks in the industry, such as the Gulf oil spill and frack-ing. But, within the sector, the oil construction and exploration stocks are more speculative, more volatile, and move ahead of the more conservative energy stocks.

All other things being equal, then, you want to overweight financial stocks at the beginning of a bull market, and you want to overweight energy stocks at the end of a bull market.

Housing Stocks

Most construction companies used to be private. But housing stocks went from virtually nothing to become a big player in the market. For example, you have the Lennars and the Hovnanians. There was nothing like that decades ago.

But now the sector has faded back into relative oblivion because residential construction has dwindled to practically nothing. Home builders are not building many homes. And the people who lent money to finance residential construction and residential housing in general are having tough times themselves. So the housing sector hasn't been an especially attractive place to be over the last couple of years; the stock prices have gone down, and their percentage of the overall market has dwindled considerably.

To participate in commercial construction, most institutional investors tend to buy materials stocks, such as lumber, concrete, and copper, rather than the builders themselves.

Cyclical Sectors

Cyclical sectors are sectors that move up and down in lockstep with the economy. The two most cyclical sectors are industrials and materials. If you think that the economy is going to boom, you want to own industrials and materials. If you think that it's going into the tank, you want to avoid industrials and materials like the plague.

Defensive Sectors

Consumer-oriented stocks—especially consumer staples—and utilities are considered to be countercyclical in nature and therefore classic defensive sectors. (When you want to hide from bad things that are happening in the stock market and the economy but still stay invested, you go to safe stocks and safe companies in areas that are affected very little by the economy; they're called *defensive sectors*.)

Utilities used to be considered a very safe place to hide. During a bear market, they would go down less than the market as a whole, although they still would go down. So they would generate relative strength in a bear market. More recently, though, environmental issues, difficulties with regulatory agencies, and assorted other problems have made many utility stocks much more speculative than they used to be (see Enron). The consumer staples sector (i.e., food, retail, personal products, etc.) is now considered to be just as defensive a sector as utilities—and perhaps even more so.

Precious metals also can behave differently, particularly gold. In the past, gold sometimes moved in a countercyclical fashion to the stock market, but it didn't and doesn't do so reliably enough to be called a true countercyclical sector. (There's also the not-insignificant problem that gold stocks don't always go up and down in conjunction with gold itself.)

Subsectors

Brokerages will sell anything they think the public will buy. This often includes funds or ETFs based on criteria related to sectors, either some subsector or sub-subsector or best of breed within a sector. Remember, though, that you are losing diversity when you get into a subsector, and quite often a narrowly focused sector will move up (and down) with almost the same volatility as a single stock.

CHAPTER 14

MONETARY INDICATORS

Bond Market

The bond market is widely considered to be a leading indicator of the stock market. But there are times when the bond market and the stock market move pretty much in lockstep together; so the bond market is not always a leading indicator. There are also times when the bond market moves counter to the stock market.

In 2009, when the stock market was going up, the bond market was going down all through that time. That, in hindsight, was not a reason to be negative on the stock market, just because the bond market was going down. So sometimes the bond market leads the stock market, and sometimes the bond market doesn't lead the stock market. And sometimes high interest rates, rising interest rates, are bullish, and sometimes they are bearish. Unfortunately, we don't always know when.

The Federal Reserve as an Indicator—"Don't Fight the Fed"

The only reliable thing about interest rates is this: When the Federal Reserve (Fed) starts to tighten monetary policy, a bear market ultimately will follow. But the timing is uncertain; sometimes a bear market starts very quickly, and sometimes it takes years. So the first time the Fed raises interest rates is not necessarily a signal to flee stocks because sometimes the Fed can raise interest rates several times before the stock market responds.

"Don't fight the Fed" means don't be excessively bullish when the Fed is trying to put the brakes on economic expansion by raising interest rates. Sooner or later, the Fed will get its way.

When the Fed lowers rates, when it eases, then a bull market almost always follows. But, again, the lead times are highly irregular. At times, the market anticipates an easing and goes up even before it occurs; at others, the economic situation and inflation problems are so deep-seated that it takes several Fed moves before the market responds.

The classic rule on Fed tightening is Edson Gould's *three steps and stumble rule*, which says that it takes three Fed tightening moves to bring down a bull market. The converse is the *two tumbles and a jump rule*, which says that the Fed has to make two loosening moves before the market reacts.

Before everyone became a Fed watcher, these rules worked very well; now they're not nearly so precise because so many investors try to anticipate them. But the basic thing to know is that, generally speaking, Fed loosening is bullish for stocks and Fed tightening is bearish.

So investors have to watch the Fed. Basically, the stock market goes up because of money coming into it. If the Fed starts restricting the money coming into the market by tightening monetary policy, the stock market ultimately will stop going up.

Economic and Monetary Indicators—Stan Berge

Stan Berge, a highly respected institutional market analyst who worked for Tucker Anthony and R. L. Day in Providence, Rhode Island, first taught me that economic and monetary indicators could be used along with technical indicators to forecast the stock market. Although most economic indicators aren't useful in forecasting the stock market (remember, the stock market itself is a leading economic indicator), there are a few that are, such as the coincident/lagging economic indicators ratio. There are also some monetary indicators that lead the stock market.

The most significant monetary indicator probably is the rate of change of the money supply. The money supply is simply the total amount of money available in the economy at a particular point in time and is measured most often by adding together the currency in circulation (the dollars you have in your pocket) and certain kinds of bank deposits (the money in your checking account). Money, of course, is the driving factor behind stock prices (to paraphrase the song from *Cabaret*, "Money money money makes the market go 'round"), so an expanding money supply is bullish for stocks and a not-so-expanding money supply isn't. There are scads of ways to track monetary factors; if you'd like to dig deeper into the subject, I have some suggestions in the Appendix.

CHAPTER 15

CONTRARIAN AND SENTIMENT INDICATORS

Sentiment indicators measure what groups of investors are doing. (Not saying—doing; talk is cheap. I always—always—watch their feet, not their mouths.) Since most groups of investors are trend followers, most sentiment indicators turn bearish when the crowd is bullish, and the media is bullish, and all the people you talk with are bullish. And then at the bottoms, the vast majority of investors are bearish. Everybody is scared and frightened, and it looks like Armageddon is at hand. This turns the sentiment indicators positive. But it is only through experience that you can get the intestinal fortitude that enables you to sell when everybody else is buying and to buy when everybody else is selling.

You can follow all sorts of indicators that measure sentiment. Unfortunately, though, all you can know ahead of time is that the bearishness will be the greatest at the bottom—you don't know exactly what that level of bearishness is going to be.

In late 2008 and early 2009, bearishness reached levels that had never been seen in our lifetimes because the market and the financial system were doing things that had never been seen before. Bear Stearns went bankrupt in March 2008, and then Lehman Brothers went under in September. The government had to bail out the financial system. The story has been well told elsewhere, but suffice it to say that the system came very close, dangerously close, to seizing up and going into a state of complete nonmovement. This drove many sentiment indicators to record extremes.

Bernard Baruch's famous quote on the Depression is always applicable during both bull and bear markets. To paraphrase: "If, at the beginning of the dot-com boom, people had told themselves that 2 + 2 still equals four, things would've been different. And in the period of utter despair, like we saw in October of 2008, and again in March of 2009, when people ask, 'Will things ever get better?' the answer is, 'They always have.'"

So a good contrarian indicator will pull you away from the current trend and signal a reversal before it happens.

The danger of contrarian investing is that you will be early.

Bob Farrell, who I worked for in the 1960s, and John Bennett, who I worked for in the 1970s, are great contrarians, and I learned to do a lot of contrarian analysis from them. It's stood me in good stead. My clients are primarily big institutional investors, who, practically speaking, have to buy into weakness if they are going to be able to buy significant positions of stock. Likewise, they have to be able to sell into strength because they have to sell significant positions of stock. So my job is to tell them to buy before the weakness turns into strength and to sell before the strength turns into weakness. The one time this doesn't work well is during an obvious bubble. During the dot-com bubble, the best money managers saw it for what it was, and most of them got out of the way—but much too early, in hindsight. Later, they told me that they were amazed by how much further it had to run.

Anticipating a reversal in trend is a much higher-risk proposition than seeing a reversal that has already happened and not being afraid to jump on. This is one of the areas where an individual investor has a very real advantage over the institutional investor.

Anecdote—Bank Trust Departments

When I was at Merrill Lynch, a blotter came out every day breaking out what Merrill Lynch customers had done the day before in terms of net buying and selling. The blotter was broken down into such things as cash accounts, which was what the general public was doing; margin accounts, which is what aggressive traders were doing; short selling and short covering; and what institutions were doing. The institutional trades then were broken down into nine subcategories. I plotted all nine of them for Bob Farrell—by hand, of course, in those days. Like any good stock analysts, we were looking for one of two classes of people: those who were always right and those who were always wrong. It mattered not which one they were so long as they were consistent.

There were only two categories of institutional investors that tended to be consistently right: One was corporations buying and selling stock, either their own or the stock of other corporations, and the other was banks, trading for their own accounts.

Most institutions, though, usually did the wrong thing at the wrong time, but not consistently enough to be helpful to us. With one notable exception.

The worst investors by far were bank trust departments. This was in 1964–1965, and I have seen absolutely nothing since then to make me think that bank trust departments are any better timers of the stock market than they were back then. They consistently do the wrong thing at the wrong time. By the time investment decisions are filtered down through committees to bank trust officers and are then implemented, it's too late. It's time to make the next decision.

This is an example of groupthink at its worst. (Another is pension fund consultants, who don't get around to implementing their decisions until it's time to make the next one. But that's a tale for another day.)

But let me add something here:

An individual investor is well situated to take advantage of good indicators. If her indicators seem to be "spot on," she can trade as soon as she gets to a phone or a laptop. Her trades won't move the market. She doesn't have to get them approved by a committee at the morning meeting. And if they are wrong, her job isn't on the line. She can sell as soon as she's noticed her mistake. This is a real advantage that professional money managers dearly wish they had.

PART VI

INVESTING 101

CHAPTER 16

SELECTING INDIVIDUAL STOCKS

If you are following a piece of the market, such as an individual stock or sector, you should track what that stock is doing relative to a larger related group as well as the price of the stock itself. (This is called *relative strength*.)

So compare a stock with a sector, a sector with an index, and an index with the broad market. Is it stronger or is it weaker than the larger group?

Look for the leaders. The leadership in a new bull market telegraphs its intentions by generating relative strength toward the end of the prior bear market. So does the leadership in an intermediate rally.

If you have a stock that is making a bottom when the market averages already have gone up 50 percent, this is not nearly as interesting as if a stock is making a bottom when the market has gone down 50 percent over the last year.

In the first case, if the market already has gone up 50 percent and you have a stock that is just now making a bottom it is way behind the market; there is a reason why it has been a wallflower for that entire 50 percent move. And usually that is more of a reason not to buy it than to buy it. In fact, that laggard stock may have as much risk as reward because all too often you get false moves in a stock that lags the market. If the stock has taken so long to respond, usually there is a reason. And usually when it does get around to responding, the risk— that it will not follow through on the upside—is much greater than in a stock that bottoms before the market does.

In the latter case, though, if the market has gone down 50 percent and the stock is making a bottom, it is fighting the decline. It is trying to make a bottom when the market is still going down. And when the market ultimately stops going down, as it always does, the stock will be in an excellent position to lead the next advance. So you have the same exact chart pattern, but you now have one that is of great interest with a great deal of potential.

Market leaders are much, much better investments than market laggards.

Individual Stocks That Will Lead

John Hammerslough, with whom I worked for a long time when he was at Shields and Company and later at Kaufman Alsberg, carried this a step further with a very simple rule that he used to identify leadership in a new bull market: Buy stocks that make new all-time highs the quickest. This rule really works—and here's why.

Let's say that the market has gone down for a considerable period of time and then starts up again. Any stock that quickly makes a new all-time high has done two very good things: (1) it has resisted the decline because it has to be close enough to its old all-time high to make a new one, and (2) it then had enough strength to get over the old high. This means that it was showing relative strength both over the preceding bear market and at the beginning of the new bull market. Any stock that makes a new all-time high at the beginning of a bull market is therefore displaying well-above-average long-term relative strength—and any stock that generates well-above-average long-term relative strength at the beginning of a bull market is very likely to lead the entire bull market.

So all you need to do at the beginning of a new bull market is to buy stocks making new all-time highs. And now, thanks to the Internet, it's easy to find them. There's a list of stocks making new all-time highs each day at www2.barchart.com/stocks/athigh.php.

There usually aren't a lot of them at the beginning of a new bull market, of course, because in order to make the new all-time high list, the stock has to trade at the best price it has traded in the last 52 weeks. If you have just started a bull market, though, most stocks are trading well below their highs of the last 52 weeks, so you won't usually have a terribly long list of stocks to study.

What John Hammerslough did, then, is to simply condense the whole concept of long-term relative strength into one simple and easy-to-apply method. And it works pretty well at the beginning of an intermediate rally, too.

Buy Them All

If you invest in individual stocks, then diversify, diversify, diversify.

Remember what Peter Lynch, the legendary manager of Fidelity's Magellan Fund from 1977 to 1990, said: "If I find 10 stocks I like, I don't know which one is going to do the best, so I buy all 10."

Technical investing works best with a diversified portfolio. Not only is there less risk, but the investor learns lessons best from decisions he has made.

Any individual stock, no matter how good the technicals look (and you may have done fundamental analysis also), is subject to the Oops factor—Oops, and the company is gone.

The company's resident genius may die. The FBI may come after the company for fraud. A rival company may introduce a better product at half the price. The company's technology suddenly may become obsolete. Its product may be declared to produce brain damage.

Now the company's robust; now it's gone.

Overseas Component

There has been a lot of talk about the merits of investing in companies with overseas exposure on the theory that while the U.S. economy may be in the doldrums, emerging markets may be faring better. But U.S. companies with overseas exposure may or may not get a market benefit from diversification.

It's hard to say, in fact, who gets their money from where anymore.

Part of the overseas investing dilemma has to do with currency valuations. In order to say that companies with overseas exposure are a better investment than companies that do not have overseas exposure, you are implicitly also making a forecast on the dollar, and the dollar is notoriously difficult to forecast. (As the old joke goes, "There are only two people on the face of the earth who know with certainty what the dollar is going to do—and I don't know which one to believe.")

There are global market exchange-traded funds (ETFs) that give investors direct overseas exposure. But you really have to forecast the currency as well as the overseas market to make an informed decision with regard to investing in them.

There Is No Stock Equivalent to Cash

A lot of professional money managers who want to take a defensive posture in equities buy stocks that they consider equivalent to cash. Cash equivalents used to be things such as AT&T and utility stocks. Today, many utilities are still cash equivalents, but not all of them. The utilities with nuclear problems and problems with rate-setting boards need to be winnowed out. And, as we saw in Chapter 13, the consumer staples sector now has joined utilities as a popular cash-equivalent sector.

These stocks used to be called *widows-and-orphans stocks* because they were reliable, and investors could depend on the price staying about the same and the dividend being constant. And that was the type of risk-adverse investor they attracted.

So professional investors would buy defensive stocks, when they did at all, to cushion themselves against market declines.

But, as it turned out, today's widows-and-orphans stocks usually go down in sync with the rest of the market—maybe not as much, but they still go down. They are not equivalent to cash.

This is another area where individual investors have a huge advantage over big money managers. When I would go into institutional accounts and suggest that they become defensive, they would often reply that they were already defensive because they had a 20 percent position in cash-equivalent stocks. I would then have to break the news to them that they were not really defensive at all and were just kidding themselves: 80 percent of their portfolio was going to go down with the market, and the other 20 percent would go down somewhat less than the market.

Individual investors have the luxury—which professional money managers dearly wish they themselves had—to get completely defensive in a hurry and then get back into the market just as quickly when the storm passes.

Avoid the Bulletin Board

I do not follow bulletin-board stocks. Number one, not a single one of my clients could buy them because if you buy 10 million shares of a 2 cent stock, you don't put a lot of money to work. Also, bulletin-board stocks tend to be extremely, extremely speculative. As an analyst, I need to follow things where there are a lot of people involved so that I can analyze mass psychology as it affects the price of the stock through supply and demand. Although many bulletin-board stocks have a lot of volume, it's concentrated in a relatively few number of participants.

Bulletin board stocks are the wild, wild west of Wall Street, and serious long-term investors should delete the e-mails and chuck the direct-mail ads touting them—unread and unopened.

CHAPTER 17

WARNING INDICATORS

Trailers

Companies aren't forever things. If you are trading individual stocks, remember that not all the stocks that underperform will come back, and historic price ranges are not always a good indicator of future price ranges.

Stocks that lead in a bull market or hold up relatively well in a bear market usually survive.

Those that trail significantly behind coming out of a bear market, though, may have problems that aren't apparent to most investors yet.

One good rule to remember is that companies whose stock prices are going up are not the ones that go out of business. (Or as I like to put it, no stock in an uptrend has ever gone bankrupt!)

Never Ignore the Second Subpoena

One of the stocks that the fund managers at Tsai Management were big into during the late 1960s was a gambling stock named Parvin-Dohrmann. The concept behind gambling stocks was that Howard Hughes had just come into Las Vegas. Since he ran straight books, that meant that the other casinos were going to have to start running straight books, too, and stop the skimming that was then commonplace. This, in turn, would mean that earnings in gambling stocks in Las Vegas were going to go up.

Parvin-Dohrmann (PRV) was a very thin stock, and about three or four money managers controlled virtually all the float. One day the analyst who covered PRV was served a subpoena because the Securities and Exchange Commission (SEC) was investigating trading in the stock. A few months later he was served another subpoena. Right about then the stock's meteoric rise crested, and it crashed and burned right back down from whence it had come. This led to my now-famous sell signal: When they serve the second sub-poena, sell.

This may sound facetious, but it's not. If there is that much smoke, there is usually a fire somewhere. One subpoena may be a random event, but if a regulatory agency serves more than one subpoena, that is usually an indication that something is rotten in the state of Denmark.

It's a better idea to get out and let the investigations continue without you as a shareholder.

This is actually called *legal risk*—that the company has fallen foul of some regulation or even has committed a crime that it is trying to hide and that the defense will affect the company's future performance.

Thanks to full disclosure rules, a subpoena has to be made public. So shareholders will know that an investigation is going on and that subpoenas have been served.

One investigation may be more or less routine, but when a second subpoena is served, things are starting to get serious. Usually there is a skeleton in everybody's closet. And by the time the authorities have served the second subpoena, they are going to find that skeleton. And whether the skeleton is where they think it is or somewhere else, they will find it.

Beware Shake-Outs

There's a concept called a *shake-out*, where smaller investors become so disgusted with a volatile and declining market that they sell—usually near the bottom—and then tell themselves that they won't get back in until they know the market has "recovered" (by which they mean after it already has gone up considerably).

It's easy to tell people not to sell at the bottom, but it's much harder to actually not do it. Emotions are very strong. Unsophisticated investors may be convinced that Armageddon is at hand (although they should keep in mind that very few Armageddon calls are ever exercised). But if they are not diversified and have a portfolio of highly volatile stocks, Armageddon indeed may be at hand for them.

Part of the problem with bottoms is that, yes, they always come back, but sometimes they go down further before they come back. And what if you have no powder to burn, that is, no uncommitted assets to invest, before the next run-up?

Even very sophisticated institutional investors have a rough time with this. It's just the nature of the beast. Remember, the smartest minds in the world may be gathered on Wall Street, but that doesn't mean they enjoy seeing the market sink or have an answer for why it does or how to avoid it. They know that overtrading—speculation—may have contributed to an overly volatile market.

The best way to deal with the shakeout is to have dealt effectively with the preceding top, leaving some dry powder for the next. Barring that, investors can only attempt to remain emotionally detached during the gut-wrenching shake-outs at the bottoms.

Anecdote—Beware Flying Computers

My office at Putnam, the Market Analysis Department, was immediately adjacent to the office of Ken Pash, who managed the Putnam Equities Fund. It was one of the most aggressive funds Putnam had.

One day in 1970, after the market had been going down for a year and aggressive growth funds had had tough going all during that time, I suddenly heard strange noises from next door. Each fund manager had a little Quotron machine on his desk, and when I went over to investigate, I found that Ken had gotten so sick and tired of the quotes that were coming over his Quotron that day that he had hurled it into his wastepaper basket with a great crash.

That was a sign that we were awfully close to the bottom. So, when investors are hurling their computers out the window in disgust, that's a good sign, usually, that we are close to a bottom.

CHAPTER 18

WILD CARDS

Unwinding the Excesses—Fallout from the Financial Crisis

The financial crisis that erupted in the United States in 2008 and 2009 is a *wild card*, a skeleton in the closet, that is not likely to go away quietly. This makes the current investment environment much different from the environment we had all been used to.

Basically, we are now in the process of unwinding financial excesses that built up for decades and decades. Deleveraging processes don't complete themselves in just a few months; it takes many years, and the repercussions can be wide ranging and unforeseen. Our banking and financial systems are still very strained. Financial stocks have been underperforming for a long time, and I suspect that they are going to continue to generally underperform. The markets are very volatile, and part of this is caused by the continued uncertainty.

The financial crisis is not over—and it may get worse.

It may be affected or extended in length by credit contraction, by inflation (or deflation), by municipal debt problems, or by overseas financial and economic problems.

A Long Credit Contraction—The Japanese Model

(*Note:* Part of this section appeared in slightly different form in the *Concord Monitor.*)

From World War II all the way up until 2007, the United States was in a credit expansionary environment. Now we are in a credit contraction environment. This has given us an environment that is more similar to our 1930s than it is to the 1970s. The problem we have as analysts is that there have been so many structural changes in the last 80 years that it is very, very hard to make direct comparisons with the 1930s.

But there is one "modern" economy with a similar pattern—and that is Japan since 1990.

Like ours, Japan's recession followed bubbles—mostly finance and real estate. Japan's markets peaked in 1989.

After that, Japan had a decade-long recession and then a "lost decade" where, basically, its economy went sideways.

During the 1990s, Japan's stock market had three great advances of more than 50 percent. After all three of those advances, though, the Japanese stock market retraced all the ground that it had gained. Since then, and until recently, the Japanese market has been very anemic. This is the lost decade.

Our stock market may be in a similar position now—which means that investment returns in stocks may be below normal for quite some time.

Japan tried to solve its market problems in several of the same ways that we are trying now—stimulus spending, low interest rates, and so on.

When you are in a credit contraction environment, though, the best thing is to recognize that the economy does take swings that are more or less natural and let the economy work itself out. But just letting nature take its course is politically unpalatable, so the political powers try to "help," and that usually just ends up extending the economic malaise.

The primary lesson our government should learn is that stimulus spending does not increase market credit. A couple of years ago, anyone could get a loan. But now it's back to, "We only lend money to people who don't need it." The fact that there is not as much credit in the economy means that there isn't as much credit supporting the economy, and that's the natural contraction. It will keep going until it has fully run its course. Artificial stimuli can do nothing more than slow it down a little.

Inflation, Hyperinflation, and Deflation

Every paper currency in the known universe has devalued over time, including the dollar. As Ron Paul keeps saying, since the Federal Reserve came into being in 1913, the dollar has lost 98 percent of its purchasing power. And the Federal Reserve's stated policy is to have slow but steady inflation, 2 percent per year. This means that by this time next year, the Fed would like to see your dollar buy 98 percent of what it can buy today.

All you need to do to see the implications of this is to take a calculator and multiply a dollar by 98 percent for every year we go out into the future: 98 percent, then 96 percent, 94 percent, and so on. Twenty years out, your dollar is going to be worth—if the Fed gets its way—about 67 cents. The government's stated policy is to make it worth less and less and less. The government wants you to spend it now, not save it for later. Because, when you spend it later, it's not going to be worth a dollar.

Let's see what this does to retirement planning. If you think you're going to need $50,000 per year now to retire, what will you need in 25 years? Take a calculator and punch $50,000 in, and then punch in 1.02, and then hit the multiplication key and the equals key 25 times. (The answer is $82,030.) Put another way, the dollar that you have today will be worth only 60 cents 25 years from now if inflation is "only" 2 percent a year during that time.

So the Fed wants a steady 2 percent inflation rate. But the Fed can't control the rate of inflation: it can affect it, but it can't control it. There are two external processes that also affect the value of money: deflation and hyperinflation—and right now they are in a struggle. The great debate is which is going to win.

The hyperinflation forces are the amount of currency that is being generated by the printing presses in Washington to combat our economic problems.

Everybody always has heard of what happened in Germany in the 1920s and wonders whether it could happen here. And everybody says no. But the government is printing money. If the government keeps on printing money, prices may start

Figure 18-1: Zimbabwe $100 Trillion Note.

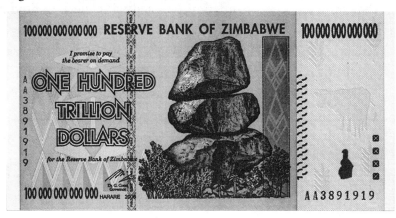

spiraling upward and get out of control, leading to *hyper-inflation*. It is exceedingly difficult to lick hyperinflation once it really starts running, as we learned in the 1970s and 1980s, when we were having double-digit inflation and double-digit interest rates—Zimbabwe found this out even more recently.

I own a Zimbabwe $100 trillion note. It's funny but tragic (Figure 18-1).

The forces of deflation are created by the deleveraging process that we are going through in unwinding the debt. This is the Japan scenario.

The danger is that once deflation spirals out of control, it is difficult to reverse it, as Japan found out over the last 20 years. No one buys, so prices drop further. And once prices start falling, everyone wants to wait to buy because everything will be cheaper in the future.

In the short term, though, we have another problem that I believe has not generated sufficient outrage and that is the effect of current monetary policy on small savers. Our 2 percent targeted rate of inflation coupled with the Fed holding down short-term interest rates to well below that is having an alarming effect on the most vulnerable in our economy, the small savers and retirees. When small savers and retirees get less than 2 percent and the government wants a 2 percent inflation rate, this imposes an extra, regressive tax on them.

Small savers and retirees, quite bluntly, are getting screwed by the Fed.

Municipal Debt, Bonds, and the Threat of Bankruptcy

Municipal debt, municipal bonds, and the threat of municipal bankruptcy should be seen as separate but interrelated issues.

Right now, people have a tendency to look at California and Illinois as the tip of an iceberg, where every municipal obligation is made of the same type of ice. But this couldn't be less true. Each municipality is different, and each municipal bond issue is different.

Right now, some muni bonds are an excellent value.

Muni bonds can be revenue bonds, construction bonds, all sorts of things—it all depends on what they are backed with and what the cash flow is of the backing authority. Project-specific bonds (i.e., not general obligation bonds) can be a good investment depending on how conservative the initial assumptions were by the issuers and how realistic the plans were. There are some very good bonds out there, going cheap.

Other muni bonds are higher risk. These are usually general obligation bonds.

General obligation bonds may depend on tax revenue projections made during a rosier environment, especially if the municipality projected that tax income not only would stay at the then-lofty levels but even increase further. But tax revenues have fallen in many places. Property taxes have fallen with property values. Income tax revenues have fallen with incomes. Sales taxes have fallen as shoppers have stopped spending. And, of course, a cranky electorate has strenuously resisted efforts to increase tax rates.

The most risky bonds are the ones issued by taxing authorities that were already stretched, that were reaching limits on the amount of debt they could safely, conservatively, issue, and then issued more anyway. Many of these may be at the flashpoint.

So there are some very good municipal bonds and some very bad ones.

Unfortunately, municipal bonds are frightfully, frightfully difficult to analyze fundamentally, and you can't do it technically because they don't trade enough to generate meaningful data. When you want to sell, the broker will make a market by bidding whatever she feels like bidding at the moment. So, if you tried to chart the price moves, you'd end up with a chart that looked like it had a bunch of little flyspecks on it.

In short, to buy municipal bonds, you have to be a fundamental analyst—and a good one. People who have the skill and take the time to study each municipal bond—and it takes a highly skilled professional going through a lot of legal documents—are salivating at the opportunities. But I stress, you have to look at each bond individually, specifically.

You can't buy a muni based on technical analysis.

Municipal bonds, however, can be bought via mutual funds. The primary attraction for investors has been their tax-free feature. So investors can diversify via a municipal bond fund and still can get tax-free yield. This is most attractive to residents of high-tax states.

The good news for the economy is that the muni bond market will not tumble like the housing securities market. Muni bonds have not been sliced and diced with other municipalities or instruments, so each one rises and falls on its own merits. So, if Monowi, Nebraska, defaults, it will be only the Monowi bonds that are hurt.

The threat that municipal bonds pose to the stock market, of course, is the ripple effect because the market is so huge ($2.7 trillion if you take state and local governments together, according to Roubini Global Economics). And the sovereign bond market—bonds of sovereign nations such as Germany and Italy—is even bigger.

If one municipality stops paying interest, the Fed may bail them out by floating short-term loans, probably at low interest rates. This, however, would only spread out and delay the problem without adding to the solution.

Right now, municipalities are governed by special laws and provisions in the tax codes. In the 1930s, during the Depression, the government moved fairly quickly to change the tax code and relax the bankruptcy law in its favor. That got the municipalities out of whatever trouble they were in at the time. They declared bankruptcy and defaulted, or threatened to, and were able to renegotiate with that as a weapon.

If that happens today, several things will happen. First, money flows will be affected significantly. Municipal bonds are bought for income, and many of them are bought by retired people.

Second, if whatever the Fed does provides significant relative advantage to those defaulting, then more and more municipalities will elect to default, creating a snowball effect.

Third, the government will have changed the provisions of existing contracts. If this is done once, the expectation will be that it can be done again. In the long run, the cost of borrowing for municipalities will go up because of the uncertainty and added risk.

Whether this happens or not may depend in part on how important the municipality is. For instance, if you're in Illinois, and Chicago wants something, Chicago usually gets it because Chicago drives the state economy. If you're in Nebraska, and Monowi wants a bailout, that's a different story. Monowi doesn't drive the Nebraska economy.

Government Debt

The United States has a huge amount of debt outstanding, and much is short term—due in one year or less. Right now we are paying 1 percent or less interest on most of our debt, when a normal interest rate would be more like 3 percent.

The debt needs to be either paid down or rolled over all the time, and those abnormally low short-term interest rates are not going to last forever. In addition, China is our biggest creditor; it's the first time in our history that we have been so far indebted to a foreign power—which means we no longer control our own destiny as much as we used to.

What happens when we hold a Treasury auction and the Chinese demand a more normal rate of interest or stay away entirely? Or ask for the debt to be denominated in yuan or another currency or a gold-equivalent value? And when the annual interest expense on the national debt triples, as it ultimately will, what will that do to our budget and our deficit?

Normally, we run up this type of debt only during wars, and we finance it domestically. The Chinese didn't finance World War II for us, and they may stop financing our current wars if they don't get a higher rate of interest to protect them against the eroding value of their dollars.

These issues are going to become more and more critical unless we get our financial house back in more stable territory.

This is long-cycle stuff, something that may not be an immediate worry but that our government should be planning for. And if it doesn't—or won't—you as an investor certainly need to.

Europe

In Europe, the amount of debt expanded to the point where it was unsustainable and now is contracting. The question is: How long will that contracting process take, and how painful will it be? Remember, we're heading into a Kondratieff winter, where the world is going from a period of exuberance, issuing debt like crazy, to a period of pessimism. Governments don't want to reduce their debt, but they are being forced to by the markets. The markets don't want to take any more debt, and they think Europe has too much debt outstanding already.

At some point, everybody—whether it be an individual or a national government—reaches a point where they simply cannot borrow any more. Many governments now have reached that point. And with the economic contraction, they don't have the revenue necessary to service the debt they already have outstanding, which is one reason why our Federal Reserve is keeping interest rates at zero.

The wild card will be if countries such as Spain or Italy, which are "too big to bail," default (or, to put it in politicians' terms, "restructure their debt"). And, of course, we are already seeing political pressure within Germany, which would be funding the bailouts.

The biggest risk may be from the uncertainty—the length of time it will take for this to shake out and resolve. It's going to be a long process.

China

When looking at charts that cover 100 years or so of data, we are always looking at the United States operating from a position of world strength. We have been the strongest, richest nation in the world since the end of World War I, and before that we were in the ascendancy.

This may be true no longer.

China's money supply is now greater than the U.S. money supply—and it has been growing fantastically fast. Over the last couple of years, China's money supply has risen 148 percent; its money supply (M2) is now $11 trillion, and ours is $9 trillion. This, of course, is why investors are worried about inflation in China—because the money supply is rising so rapidly. It's put a tremendous pressure on prices, and it explains why people are so upset about the yuan against the dollar.

If current trends continue, China will become the world's dominant economy.

Six or seven years ago, Dean LeBaron recalled what somebody from the Chinese financial hierarchy told him: "In 50 years, the Chinese are going to have American house boys." It seemed crazy when I first heard it six or seven years ago—but it doesn't seem quite so crazy now.

And 25 years ago, would you have believed that U.S. market analysts were going to have to study the Chinese stock market? But we do, because it is starting to drive the global economy. When you look at the global stock market, China is a major sector—and it drives the whole Pacific Rim.

Real growth over the next 50 years, then, is more likely to come from China and other emerging markets than from the United States. The Chinese stock market, though, is pretty frothy, and it's difficult for outsiders to buy pure Chinese stocks. In fact, there are really two Chinese stock markets: Chinese stocks that foreigners can buy and Chinese stocks that only the Chinese can buy. And these two markets go in two different directions sometimes. In addition, there is a lot more hanky-panky in the Chinese market—a *lot* more—than many investors should be comfortable with.

PART VII

ADVICE FOR THE PERPLEXED

CHAPTER 19

WHAT TO BUY WHEN THE MARKET'S FALLING

Chances are that you are primarily an equities investor or will use this book to help manage an equities portfolio. But during a secular bear market—or during a Kondratieff winter— is there anything else that you can do—especially with the financial markets being so much more volatile than usual?

This may not be an academic question for the next few years. *Barron's* says, "1982–2000 was the cycle of financial assets, and so from now through 2016 or 2018, hard assets should do better than financial assets, theoretically. But commodities stocks, cyclical stocks, are very volatile."

There are three traditional strategies in a down financial market: (1) Stay in cash or buy cash equivalents, (2) buy stocks that are considered "defensive," and (3) buy hard assets, such as real estate, commodities, and precious metals.

Cash

The conventional wisdom is that cash doesn't hold its value because the inflation rate is higher than the rate on money-market accounts.

On the other hand, if you get bona fide deflation, that is, if real estate keeps going down, if the stock market is vulnerable, if gold responds to deflationary pressures, if there is no money to be made anywhere, then cash, even if it loses its purchasing power to a small extent, is a better place to be than any alternative.

But cash usually isn't that attractive because there are so many different investment vehicles available now. Some years ago, at an American Association of Professional Technical Analysts brainstorming session, Hal Marlow, who was successfully managing money by shifting back and forth between exchange-traded funds (ETFs), was asked, "Don't you ever go to cash?" And he said no; thanks to all the varied ETFs, there was always something, somewhere doing well.

There is a wide range of ETFs in the overseas markets, for example, and it's rare that every single investment vehicle in the world goes down at the same time.

Defensive Stock Sectors—Looking for Relative Strength

Classic defensive stocks are stocks that are a lot less volatile than the market and thus are considered a relatively safe place to hide.

They are also often countercyclical, as discussed earlier.

During a bear market, however, even though defensive stocks often go down less than the market as a whole, they still go down. Relative strength in a bear market just means that your stock is going down less than the market as a whole.

I have never understood why it is a good thing for a money manager to go to a client and say, "Well, the market averages were down 13 percent last year, but your account was only down 9 percent. We beat the market by 4 percent!" Maybe so—but you still have 9 percent less in your account than you started the year with.

Utilities used to be the classic defensive sector; their prices didn't move much in either direction. But now, as I said earlier, you have to watch out for nuclear energy problems and regulatory problems. Stick to a fund, or chose your utility stocks carefully. Consumer staple stocks also go down less than the market. But they, too, still go down.

Real Estate

The traditional way for the average person to participate in hard assets is through owning real estate. And the more working class you are, the more your home is likely to be your major asset or even your only significant asset. And because you live there, you are likely to spend weekends adding value through labor—through remodeling, painting, or putting on a new roof. These are all good things.

But a house is not primarily an investment; it's a place to live. Home owners didn't believe that for a while.

Real estate recently went through a period of irrational exuberance the likes of which have never been seen before in the United States. It created a secular peak in real estate in 2006–2007, and the real estate market now is working off the excesses associated with that secular peak. And so, because there are long-term corrective forces working against investors in the real estate market, that classic physical asset is not as good an alternative as it was.

Most of the problem in the real estate market has been from simple speculation. People were buying houses they couldn't afford in the expectation that prices would rise so fast that they would be able to sell at a profit. That worked for a short time, and a mania was born.

Normally, owner-occupied houses never should be considered primarily as an investment. They are illiquid. They depreciate. Carrying costs are astronomical. Plus, the desirability of any one house can change. What happens if you redecorate, but you have poor taste? If a garage band moves in next door?

Another problem with selling real estate is that most buyers calculate the price as an all-in monthly payment. But the monthly costs also involve other things than mortgage principal and interest—property taxes, utility costs, insurance, and other recurring expenses, any of which can rise owing to any number of factors.

Our current state and local budget crises mean that property taxes are likely to rise. Rising energy costs affect all prices, but they will affect the prices of homes, especially where energy costs are significant.

Well, if real estate taxes double, and energy costs double, and insurance costs double, the value of your house may go down quite a bit because affordability is tied to the all-in monthly payment. Your local municipality or your local energy company may appropriate a chunk of your house's value, and there's nothing you can do about it.

But the most important price determinant right now is probably market sentiment. And that sentiment is negative.

Buyers on the whole expect that prices will fall further, that interest rates eventually will rise, that property taxes will go up, that foreclosed properties will continue to be a negative factor, that energy will continue to get more expensive, that housing construction will get more energy efficient, that family size will shrink, and a host of other things that are negative for the prebuilt single-family home.

And because people typically have to stay in homes for a while and investments are long-term, the inferences are especially negative.

One decision that people usually don't make, but should, is the decision on whether to buy or rent. Clearly, in hindsight, the best decision that somebody could've made in 2007 was to sell their house and start renting. Because, if they sold their house in 2007, they sold it at the high. And if they rent until house prices stop falling, they are actually gaining money relative to all the home owners around them. It's certainly something worth considering. Just because it is the American dream to own a house doesn't mean that it's the thing that everybody in America should do.

On the other hand, if inflation goes up, house prices may stabilize or even rise. This isn't necessarily good, though. If an average house costs $200,000, and by the time you retire the average house costs $500,000, you might not like the world you find yourself in. Gas could be $20 per gallon. Or a loaf of generic white bread could be $10, and you'll think twice before you get one. And a doctor's visit could be $800. And the price of gold could be $5,000 per ounce.

And that might not make you happy.

Commodities—General Characteristics

Commodities can be countercyclical, but watch out for them. In terms of sentiment, they perform the opposite of financial assets.

That is, when prices rise, they very often rise on fear owing to a perceived shortage. So commodities tops can be very volatile and very brief. Commodities bottoms usually reflect low and/or stable prices. Commodities bottoms are like financial asset tops. They are usually protracted, rounded, gentle things.

Agricultural commodities are a play on rising food prices. If you are bullish on agricultural prices, other than buying agricultural commodity ETFs, which are not really viable investment alternatives for most of us, you are forced to buy stocks in fertilizer companies, seed companies, and other alternatives.

Gold

Gold is sometimes considered countercyclical (See Figure 7-7). But it hasn't been of late.

The problem is that gold is not purely a physical asset. It is also the most traditional long-term store of value. So sometimes, not often, but sometimes, physical assets can do well, and gold does not do as well. And at other times, gold can do well while other physical assets don't.

Traditionally, gold has been a long-term investment—a way to transfer wealth between generations. For example, say that you have $100,000 and you want to pass it along to the next generation. History tells you that the $100,000 cash will be worth a lot less when it is handed down to the next generation, whereas $100,000 in gold will be worth the same in purchasing power and much more in dollars. So gold preserves wealth. It's really as much a defensive investment as it is an offensive investment.

You're anticipating a currency devaluation, in other words. And you're also anticipating that gold will continue to be perceived as the best alternative to paper currency. In essence, buying gold is a vote of no confidence in the currency. (As Ian McAvity, a highly regarded gold analyst, has said, "The question to ask is not how high is gold going to go; the question to ask is how low is the dollar going to go.")

In the long term, this has been a very good bet. Since 1913, the dollar has lost 98 percent of its purchasing power. The Federal Reserve has a stated policy of inflating at the rate of roughly 2 percent per year. It doesn't take too much time with a calculator to figure out that if you have a dollar, and it loses 2 percent of purchasing power each year, it is not going to buy you a heck of a lot in 25 years—only 60 percent of what it will buy today, in fact.

Some gold bugs have said that they see gold going to $5,000 per ounce, but then add that if it does, you may not like the world you're living in when it gets there. You take your $5,000 gold and buy gas for $25 a gallon. On the other hand, if you've got some extra money and you want to try to preserve its buying power, gold is a good place to be.

Part of the attraction of gold is that you can store it in a relatively small space. As my friend Dean LeBaron has said jokingly, it is very easy to diversify a gold portfolio— just bury it in more than one backyard.

Gold is currently in a secular bull market. When that bull market is over, gold is likely to turn down sharply. Gold is not likely to run to wherever it is going to go—and I will pick a number out of the air—$2,500. Gold is highly unlikely to run to $2,500 and then go back and forth between $2,200 and $2,500 over a period of several years, building a big top prior to a decline back toward $1,000. When gold stops going up, it is likely to make a very small reversal pattern on the chart, spend a relatively short time building the top, and then turn back down. (When it hit its multidecade peak of $850 in January 1980, in fact, it reversed in just a single day!)

Gold bottoms are also different. When gold has bottomed in the past, it usually built a fairly lengthy bottom, and it took a long, long time for the bottom to develop completely.

Uranium, Copper, Other Metals, Raw Materials

Industrial commodities are another investment alternative.

Some people who are supposed to be knowledgeable about these things claim that the most undervalued physical asset right now is uranium, which became even more undervalued after the Fukushima disaster. But this depends on what happens to nuclear energy.

But industrial commodities are also very, very risky.

Other raw materials, such as lumber and so on, fit in peripherally with precious metals. Usually, if precious metals are going up, then raw materials are going up, too.

For most investors, though, investing in industrial commodities—if you do it at all—is best done through mining stocks.

Mining Stocks

Mining stocks are a financial asset that tracks the price of the underlying commodity more than the financial asset market.

John Maurice, one of Putnam's legendary fund managers, always claimed that mining stocks led the underlying commodity. Gold mining stocks, in other words, supposedly turn up and down ahead of gold itself. I haven't tested this statistically, but from an observational standpoint, it certainly seems to work. In other words, mining shares usually start up before the metal itself, and mining shares usually stop going up before the metal itself.

But I emphasize the word *usually.*

Precious metals analysts always have a field day analyzing major mining stocks and particularly gold mining stocks. Obviously, if the price of gold goes up, the value of the gold reserves, of the gold that is sitting in the ground to be mined, goes up. And therefore, the value of gold mining shares goes up. But it's not always a one-to-one correlation. Also, one of the signs of a peak in the price of precious metals is when very speculative mining stocks start getting very active.

Anecdote—Gold Fever

Gold first went over $200 an ounce in the late 1970s; it had gotten to $200 a few years earlier but had backed off, and it was now going up again. Some of the people at Putnam decided to buy gold stocks in their own accounts. They asked me to call Ian Notley, a very gifted market analyst in Toronto whom I worked with, and ask him what the most speculative Canadian gold mining stock was. Ian laughed, and laughed, and laughed. And he finally said, it's probably Québec Sturgeon River.

Well, this was very definitely not a stock the people at Putnam could buy in a fund, but they could—and did—buy it in their own accounts. But since they had all been educated at the Harvard Business School, they wanted to do things just like they had been taught at the "B School."

For instance, they noticed that Québec Sturgeon River's annual shareholders' meeting was coming up. They thought that one of them probably should attend it because they now had built up fairly sizable positions in the stock. So I called my friend Ian in Toronto, and he started laughing again. He said, "They can come up here, if they want to, but they should be aware of two things. One, the annual meeting probably will be held in the anteroom of a lawyer's office, and two, it probably will be conducted in French."

The point is, when the Québec Sturgeon Rivers of the world start moving, when interest has gone past the more established mining stocks such as Newmont and filtered down to the most speculative strata of gold mining stocks, then the run-up is getting toward the end.

Art

The problems with housing may explain why there is so much interest in art these days. Major artworks are selling at record prices, as are stamps and other collectibles.

But the problem with those real assets is that it's so hard to buy them.

If the only person who was ever always right got on television and said, "I think financial assets are going to do well over the next 10 years," it would be easy to follow his advice because financial assets are so easy to buy. Just run out and buy stocks, bonds, and so on. But if that same person, who was always right, said, "I think physical assets are going to do well over the next 10 years," it's not easy to go and take advantage of that. It's not easy to buy physical assets.

What if you don't know a Masaccio from a Monet from a Mondrian? If all 2 cent stamps look like they're worth 2 cents?

And how do you dispose of all this stuff quickly when the time comes to get away from hard assets and back to financial assets?

CHAPTER **20**

MANIAS, PANICS, AND BUBBLES

How to Spot a Top in a Fad Group— Initial Public Offerings (IPOs)

Fad groups are created when investors get irrationally exuberant about a particular group for some reason or other. The stocks go bananas, and Wall Street's investment bankers rush companies in the group to market via initial public offerings (IPOs). Everyone seems to think that those IPOs can do no wrong and wants to get in on them; everyone thinks that it will make them rich.

Usually, the stocks belong to an industry that is touted as the "next best thing." Very often, the first couple of IPOs do very well, and everybody gets, if not rich, at least richer. Google comes to mind right now.

While I was at Putnam in the 1970s, Ron Sadoff, an analyst from Milwaukee who now heads a money-management firm there, taught me the way to recognize a top in a fad group.

Back then, he was talking about mobile home construction or double-knit socks, but the recent levitations in LinkedIn and Yandex brought his top-identification rule to mind once again.

Ron Sadoff's rule is simple:

"When an IPO in a fad group trades below its offering price on settlement day, the fad has run its course."

The logic here is that when settlement day comes (which, currently, is in three days), the free ride for people who got in on the IPO is over—and if people taking advantage of the free ride aren't making money at that time, it's a clear indication that the game in that particular fad group is over.

Please note that the stock has to sell below its *offering* price on settlement day to trigger Ron's rule—not its opening price, which may be substantially higher.

Sadoff's fad group top rule is something to keep in the back of our minds as other big Internet IPO's follow LinkedIn and Yandex to market.

(And yes, I know that market players aren't supposed to get free rides. Guidelines and rules get bent a lot on Wall Street, though.)

Bubbles and Rolling Bubbles

Bubbles and rolling bubbles aren't good. They concentrate investment capital in a particular asset or class of assets, and they create emotional swings that affect the broad market. They used to occur pretty infrequently but have been taking place more and more often in recent years.

The two biggest ones recently were the "tech wreck" in 2001 and the housing bubble in 2006.

The "tech wreck" I discussed earlier. There was a giddy sense that "this time was different," that technology was going to make such fundamental improvements to human efficiency that we could all retire with a $200,000 investment. Returns for a while were way up into the double digits.

It's been said that the four worst enemies of a successful investor are hope, fear, greed, and vanity. In this case, it was greed and then hope. Many unsophisticated investors got in at the tail end of the technology bubble (after the news had convinced them that the market increases were real and would be sustained into the indefinite future) and then refused to believe otherwise, even when the market took a nosedive. They got in near the top and couldn't get out of the way when it started to fall.

The housing bubble is harder to explain. It was not based on hope; it was based on something more akin to a Ponzi scheme. As long as there were more buyers than sellers, prices would go up. The buyers and sellers created each other—everyone was trying to "buy up" at the same time. The psychology was that housing prices had never fallen—and therefore they would never fall. (I used to tell people that if this were indeed the case—if housing prices would, indeed, never fall—Fidelity would take its more than $1 trillion under management and invest every single dollar in residential real estate. Fidelity didn't because it simply wasn't true.)

The crazy thing is that some people think that this is still applicable; once prices stop falling, there will be a leveling off, and then prices will start going up again. Well, they may—or they may not. Remember inflation. Will house prices increase, or will everything else go up faster, and the value of the dollar decrease? It may not be a world you will be happy living in.

Housing first must fill its purpose as an affordable home for working people.

Again, as I mentioned earlier, there is a long-term swing between financial assets and real assets. There is a logical time to buy real estate, and that is usually during a structural bear market. But right now, real estate prices are still too high in all too many areas, and the market is still too chaotic as lending institutions try to get rid of all the properties on which they've had to foreclose. In addition, a lot of people are choosing to rent and are putting their money to better use elsewhere.

Housing Securities

One way to tell that you're in a bubble is when there is so much demand for financial vehicles in a certain area that Wall Street falls all over itself creating them and bringing them to market—and starts making boatloads of money from them in the process. Wall Street is real good at doing things like that. Take the example of housing-backed securities. Demand for these outstripped production of viable mortgages. Originators needed mortgages to package. So they sent out people to originate mortgages, and they said, "We don't care what they look like; we just need mortgages. You give us the mortgage, we will package it and sell it." So there was this huge demand for mortgages. And the standards for mortgages went to zero.

That expanded the housing bubble.

The cart pulled the horse. Demand for a financial product (mortgages) far outstripped the supply of them (sound mortgages, that is).

240

When there is a great demand for some sort of investment, whether it be dot-com stocks in 2000 or mortgage vehicles in 2006 and 2007, Wall Street will gladly (and very profitably) create that investment vehicle—but it's usually the sign of at least the beginning of the end. Whenever people start packaging things like that, whenever it becomes ubiquitous—and I don't mean people hawking gold on late-night television; I mean people selling big chunks of investments to huge investors—then a top is approaching.

I used to tell Herb Emilson, who was the head of mutual fund sales at Putnam, that when things were good for him, they were bad for me, and vice versa. By that I meant that if it was easy for his salespeople to sell, say, aggressive growth funds, it probably was a bad time to buy them from a long-term standpoint. But if the salespeople had to take clients to a bar, get them drunk, and then pull a loaded revolver on them to get them to buy those aggressive growth funds, well, that was usually a pretty good time to buy them.

Always remember: "When the time comes to buy, you won't want to."

Conversely, if Wall Street is bullish on it and making boatloads of money on it, it's either over or about to be over.

Panic "Waves"—Changes in Investor Behavior

We've talked a lot about investor behavior. Have you seen a change in investor behavior over the last, say, 20 years?

As Bob Farrell has said, "History does not repeat itself exactly, but behavior does."

Investor behavior changes over long periods of time in cyclical fashion. By that I mean that the public is, at times, very involved in the stock market, as in the 1920s, the late 1960s, and the late 1990s and early 2000s. And at times they are relatively inactive in the stock market, as in the 1930s and 1940s and in the 1970s and early 1980s.

And that is starting to be the case again. The average investor is becoming more and more disenchanted with the stock market, thanks to below-average returns and the extreme price gyrations caused by high-frequency traders and hedge funds, and is looking for alternate investments.

So, although investor behavior has changed compared with what it was 10 years ago, it hasn't changed compared with what it was in the late 1970s or the 1930s. At the moment, the pendulum that swings between an unusually involved public and an unusually inactive one is swinging toward unusually inactive but has not gotten anywhere near the past extremes in that regard yet.

CHAPTER 21

WALL STREET IS NOT YOUR FRIEND

Wall Street has changed greatly in the last 50 years in two respects. First, the role of stock issuance has changed from need to reward. Second, the role of the investor has changed from investor to speculator—and sometimes from speculator to gambler.

The Changing Role of Stock Issuance— From Need to Reward

In the olden days, selling stock was a way of raising venture capital. Let's say that John Smith comes up with an idea for a new venture, a company to make widgets, but he needs capital, so he creates Smith's Widgets. He goes around and tries to get people to invest money in his company. He sells shares. And, as Smith's Widgets starts to take on more and more market share, as it grows, it will sell more shares along the way to raise capital.

Well, not everybody who bought Smith's Widgets stock from the offering wants to hold it forever. They need to have a place to sell it, and that's why things like the New York Stock Exchange (NYSE) and the Nasdaq exist. These are places where individual investors can buy and sell "used" stocks and can build a position in common stocks.

So, although the economic reason that stock is issued in the first place is to raise capital for new ventures, the stock market's real meaning in life is as a postoffering venue to give investors who participated in the capital-raising stage a place to sell their shares when they want.

It seems to me, though, that the reason many companies go public has changed. No longer do companies need the money that going public brings them. Now going public just means that the original investors cash in on the company's success. Those investors—the well-connected venture-capital firms who got in on the ground floor before the public ever had a chance to buy—are made rich. Very, very rich.

Remember, too, that once a company has the money from an offering, trades on the stock market are meaningless as far as it is concerned. When a share of Microsoft trades, for example, it has nothing whatsoever to do with Bill Gates. It's just people selling stock that they had bought at some point from somebody else. Microsoft doesn't get a penny out of it anymore.

But it's the stock from those original offerings that is ultimately sold, and resold, and resold. So the stock market is really nothing more than a used stock market. When you buy a stock, you just get a piece of paper that's been traded over and over and over again—and is just looking for a happy home where it can live for more than just a few seconds.

Underwriting Fees—The Drug of Investment Banks

The biggest money on Wall Street is made through underwriting fees. If Wall Street comes up with a new product and sells it, the sellers make a lot more money than if they sell an existing product from the marketplace. If somebody goes and buys or sells 100,000 shares of Microsoft through Goldman Sachs, that generates only a small commission. But if Goldman Sachs sells an initial public offering (IPO) on Facebook, it'll get an underwriting fee amounting to 2 or 3 percent of the deal. It's exorbitant. It's huge. So every time Wall Street's financial engineers come up with some fancy new product, they take about a 2 percent cut when they go out and persuade people to buy it.

And the only thing Wall Street cares about with regard to these IPOs or new products is whether it can sell them. Wall Street doesn't invent new products to benefit investors—it does so because it thinks it can sell them and earn huge underwriting fees. The phrase *putting lipstick on a pig* is all too often appropriate in these cases.

Always remember—underwriting fees are where the really, really big bucks on Wall Street are made.

Complexity in the Bond Market

In the past, investors bought bonds. Now they can buy all sorts of other things, such as credit default swaps. The more sophisticated the new investment vehicles are, the less investors are able to understand them, and the bigger are the underwriting fees that Wall Street can charge. If Wall Street's financial engineers can put mortgages in a big pot and then slice them and dice them, instead of just taking the mortgage and selling it, they can charge you for the slicing and dicing. And believe me, they do.

As it turns out, though, Wall Street wasn't very good at the slicing and dicing, and the rating companies were even worse with their ratings because the AAA-rated tranches turned out to be not much better than the much, much more speculative B-rated ones. Wall Street had created Frankenstein monsters of securities. However, as long as the sellers could convince people to buy them, and as long as there was a good yield on them, they were bought. And that was the problem: Investors bought them for the perceived better yield, and the risk involved in that better yield was hidden by their complexity.

Brokers would say, "You can only get 4 percent in regular AAA paper, but here's our new AAA MBS CES [or whatever they called it], where you can get 5.25 percent." Wow.

Ray deVoe, whom I knew back in the days when he was at Spencer Trask, says "More money has been lost reaching for yield than at the point of a gun." The folks who bought all those higher-yielding AAA things that were really just pieces of junk now know this all too well.

Mutual Fund or a Private Account?

Here's something that may surprise you: I think that investors in mutual funds are better off than investors who have a multi-million-dollar account with the same management company.

Here's why.

Let's say that you are on a plane, and the person sitting next to you manages a mutual fund. He's thinking about the fund, thinking about his current holdings, and thinking about his next picks. If his performance has been poor, he's thinking about how to improve it; if it's been good, he's thinking about keeping it that way. The point is, he's devoting 100 percent of his attention to the mutual fund he's managing.

But if the person sitting next to you is a pension fund manager, she's traveling with one of her firm's salespeople. They're thinking about the client they're going to meet with and whether that client will be happy or not. How will they spin the meeting? Is the presentation package in order? Unlike the mutual fund manager, the pension fund manager's attention is focused on the relationship with the client—not the portfolio.

And that's why I say that you get the most bang for your buck with a mutual fund.

Choosing a Broker

Choosing a broker is just as important as choosing a doctor. You wouldn't choose a doctor just because he was friendly and took you out to lunch once in a while, and you shouldn't choose a broker that way either.

Pick someone who is professional and treats your relationship that way. Also, pick someone who isn't shy about telling you exactly what their responsibilities will be regarding your account. Will she actively manage it? Will she attempt to time the market? How many clients does she have? What is her commission structure? And if your broker recommends a fund, ask about its load fees (sales charges).

Ponzi Schemes

There's an old rule: "If something on Wall Street sounds too good to be true, it is." In the late 1990s, a local guy by the name of Len Bogdan told people that he could deliver guaranteed, perfectly safe 12 to 14 percent returns when the going interest rate was only 8 percent. We all knew it couldn't be done. There's no possible way to do it. My wife even sent a letter to the owners of the local radio station, where Bogdan had a paid weekly program, warning the station that what Bogdan was promising to do couldn't be done—at least not legally. Well, it turned out that he was doing it through a Ponzi scheme, and the guy's now in jail. But retirees were so desperate for income that they were vulnerable to pitches like that.

The sales pitch goes something like this: "Come on. We know the average investor isn't getting any money from his bank; he's not getting it from rolling CDs over. And we've got this thing that's perfectly safe—and gives you yield." Well, if it gives you a higher yield than the market rate, it's not safe. Not at all. There's no way that it can be safe. The only ways that you can get a yield that's above the current market rate are (1) to take on more risk (the debt of a small retail operation is riskier than that of Walmart) or (2) to make a longer-term investment (a 30-year bond in a company is riskier than three-month commercial paper issued by the same company).

There's another old rule: "Ecce homo!" That's Latin for "Take a good look at the guy." Bernie Madoff scammed many people, but many others saw right through him. How did Bernie spend his time? He socialized! He spent money! That's all he cared about. He wasn't working on managing money.

CHAPTER 22

HAS WALL STREET CHANGED INVESTING INTO GAMBLING?

Investing, Speculating, and Gambling

If you consider the spectrum of investments, from bona fide investing through speculation to gambling, where do some so-called investments fall?

I'm always amazed to see things called "investments" and practices called "investment practices" when they are really speculations that are very close to gambling, if not gambling itself. Look in the media—they will say that such and such a hedge fund has taken a position that the euro will fall. The hedge fund isn't investing in the euro declining—it's just making a bet that it will. And a lot of the activity on Wall Street these days is really nothing more than gambling. A lot of the hedge fund activity is gambling. They're betting. They might say that they are speculating, but where does one draw the line in speculating versus gambling and in investing versus speculating?

The risks obviously are higher as you move from investing to speculation and as you move from speculation to gambling.

Some of the instruments that people thought were AAA-rated investments turned out to be gambling instruments. And unfortunately, they were so tied to the banking and credit system that they darn near brought the system down. It brought down a number of big players in the financial system—and almost brought the system down.

And it would have, too, without a bailout. And who paid for the bailout? You and me. And who got the benefit of the bailout? Them! And they're still living the good life while you and I are still working hard to pay our taxes.

But we won't go there.

The question, of course, is whether those who have sinned have learned their lessons or whether they have learned that if they screw things up, the government will come along and help out, and therefore, they might as well take bigger chances than they otherwise would because the downside is not as big as it otherwise would be. You and I screw up with a mortgage, and we lose our house. The bank screws up with millions of them, it gets bailed out.

Wall Street Enables Gambling—Facebook

One of the things Wall Street does really well is create instruments for people to speculate or gamble with. (Not invest—speculate or gamble.) One game we saw recently involved Facebook. Facebook can't have more than 500 investors without having to disclose certain financial information, which it does not want to do yet. But Facebook wanted some money. So Goldman Sachs went out and created a vehicle that invests in Facebook, and a lot of investors then invested in it. So now we have a lot of investors investing in Facebook through Goldman's vehicle. It circumvents the intent of the law, but everybody looks the other way and gets away with it—until something backfires, something blows up, and then somebody gets bailed out again.

And somebody else gets scapegoated.

EVERYTHING ELSE

CHAPTER *23*

RULES TO LIVE BY

Over the years, I've had many people ask me what I think the most important rules are to investing. I've always responded that some of the most basic investing rules could apply to just about anything in life; some are old adages, and only a few are new or surprising.

Bob Farrell's rules (see Chapter 3) are the best place to start. Here are a few other suggestions.

Document Your Important Decisions

Document each buy or sell decision that you make. The best way is on paper. The second-best way is to save screenshots in a static format (PDF or PostScript, for instance, or through the screen capture feature). Write a paragraph to go with each screenshot. Save it in a folder. Name the folder something logical (such as "YYYYMMDD Stock Decision—20090630 Apple buy"). When you sell the stock, analyze that decision also ("Sector declining" or "Major top spotted" is adequate).

Too many times people say, "Well, I follow the *Fubar Report*, and it said to buy OverboughtDotCom." Well, *Fubar* didn't make the decision for you—you made it yourself. If you use some report, document why you believed the report's conclusion was correct.

Once every six months, prepare a summary report and explain your investment decisions to another human being. (Not your dog—another human being.) Just knowing that you will have to do this will make a big difference in how you operate.

Learn to Think Visually

People ask me how I am able to keep so many charts in my head, and I ascribe some of it to the training I received (and gave myself) at the Manhattan Fund before the age of computers (Figure 23-1).

Most people think of computers as a minor miracle, a limitless font of information. I don't disagree with this. But now try to imagine being inside a computer, having charts everywhere you look.

At the Manhattan Fund, we sat in the middle of gigantic amounts of information, everywhere we looked, and each bit of information was important enough for us to compile and plot by hand.

A long counter ran the length of the room. It faced the big quotation board and the New York Stock Exchange (NYSE) and American Stock Exchange (AMEX) tickers.

Our 3- by 3-foot notebooks, which contained individual stock information, sat on that counter.

Our "history book" was on the back shelf. At the end of each year, the *New York Times* published a chart of the market over

Figure 23-1: Gerry Tsai and the Author in the Manhattan Fund Chart Room.

An introduction

Managing money has always posed formidable challenges. But never more so than today. Money needs constant attention in this era when taxation compounds, inflation robs the dollar of purchasing power, and technology obsoletes seemingly excellent investment opportunities.

The need for constant investment attention has intensified in today's complicated, sophisticated money market. The increasing market influence of large institutional investors, the growth of the "over-the-counter" market, the development of technological opportunities . . . each contributes to the difficulty one has in managing money today. For that reason, many individuals and institutions with funds entrust the responsibility for their money management to professional investment counselors.

Tsai Investment Services, Inc. is a professional investment counselor, registered under the Investment Advisers Act of 1940.

This booklet concerns itself with the challenge of investment counseling . . . and with the ability of Tsai Investment Services, Inc. to successfully meet that challenge.

the past year, annotated with the major events that happened during the year. We sent somebody over to the New York Public Library on 42nd Street to copy those charts going back as far as we could. So not only could we see the market in 1950, but we also could see the events that happened during 1950 that affected the market. It was an invaluable reference.

The walls in the chart area were covered with layers of charts. Against one wall were 25 chart panels that flipped, like pages of a book, so we had 50 big panels of charts to look at.

Against the opposite wall there were three layers of sliding panels, for a total of 12 panels' worth of information. This is where the most important charts were located. We had all the main charts that technical analysts use, but we also had charts for currencies, the bond market, short-term interest rates, and supply-demand ratios.

You got a memory jog from each chart. If you weren't 100 percent familiar with the chart, it became familiar bit by bit because you were always looking at the same chart. (With the computer, this is not quite the same; you can call up charts, but you are always looking at a somewhat different chart.)

Of course, today, paper charts wouldn't be used. It took three people working a combined total of about 20 hours a day just doing calculations and plotting them to keep up all our charts. Back then, that's what state of the art was. (Now, it's at Fidelity; they just installed the world's biggest LCD screen in their Chart Room so that they can show up-to-the-second computer-drawn charts to a whole roomful of money managers and analysts.)

Ignore the News

I mentioned earlier that the market leads the news and that, therefore, you should not base trading decisions on the news. There are other reasons to avoid financial news shows, too.

Always remember that the financial media is in the business of getting you to watch or listen to them as much as possible—which means they have to be short-term oriented, and they have to be entertaining. And both those traits can be hazardous to your wealth.

If the market sells off between 2 and 2:30 p.m. during the day, for example, this can be very important to people on trading desks. And it is likely to be something that is discussed at great length on financial television shows. But it should have absolutely no influence on a long-term investor.

If you are watching financial television, be aware that the shows with the most consistent viewerships are the "fear" and "greed" shows that highlight pundit opinions that things are going to get much worse or much better. Remember, too, that fear is a stronger emotion than greed.

Meanwhile, life goes on. The megapatterns that long-term investors should focus on are discernible only with distance, and watching minute-by-minute developments makes them much, much harder to focus on.

Ignore the Day-to-Day Market Noise

A minute-by-minute chart can show a lot of swings during the day, and not a single one of them is of any concern or significance to a long-term investor.

For example, very often the market will make a move right at the close. News reporters may try to attach some significance to this, but often the real reason is very benign. The late Mike Epstein, who worked on trading desks and the NYSE floor for many decades, explained it this way: "If you have an order that you are working on during the day, let's say a large sell order, and you are selling the stock in dribs and drabs all during the day, but it comes to be 15 minutes before the close and you haven't completed it, what you'd like to do is to continue working the order the next day. But you don't know whether you'll get the order the next day. You have it today, and you may not have it tomorrow. So the idea is to work the order as much as you can for the rest of the day because you may not see it tomorrow." So a lot of the gyrations right at the close are people trying to clean up buy and sell orders that they were working on during the day. There may not be any carryover whatsoever the next morning.

Even moves that have some significance to the market may not have significance for a small investor. If you get up in the morning and the Standard & Poor's (S&P) futures are up or down 12 points, the market is going to lurch one way or the other at the open. Institutional investors who are in the game have the computer power to take advantage of this in a split second. But an individual investor will be too late. So he has to step back from the noise and focus on the long-term moves in the market.

Many trading packages and investment books describe how to play in the noise, how to trade on a very short-term basis, and describe tools that are used on a very short-term basis.

Technically savvy long-term investors, though, have to step back and look at the full picture—look at the forest rather than the individual trees. Or perhaps more apropos, look at the forest rather than the individual leaves on the individual trees.

Be an Investor—Not a Trader

I've said it before: Buy for the longer term. A June 2011 poll by the American Association of Individual Investors (AAII) asked: "How often do you check your portfolio value?"

Daily: 57 percent
Weekly: 29 percent
Quarterly: 8 percent
More when the market is up: 4 percent
More when the market is down: 2 percent

Be Skeptical

Bob Edwards, the best investor at Tsai Management, taught me the importance of skepticism (Figure 23-2). People from Wall Street were constantly pitching him ideas (we called

Figure 23-2: Walter Deemer and Bob Edwards.

them "stories"). He'd heard them all and tried to poke holes in every one. He was almost always successful. But when he wasn't, he bought the stock.

Bill Moyers put it slightly differently in a recent interview on the *Jon Stewart Show*: "Everyone wants to give his opinion. It's the facts they are trying to hide."

Be Cheerful When Others Are Fearful

Remember that at the bottom of the market volatility will be high, and all the news will be bad because the news programs will attempt to explain the low/volatile market through recent events. But that's when you should be looking for a bottom, for a buy signal.

Of course, the reverse is also true. Be fearful when others are cheerful. When all the news is good and the market is complacent, there's often a storm ahead.

Don't Overtrade

Never overtrade. Resist the temptation, even though it's so easy to do now. You can trade stocks on the Internet without even making a phone call. And commissions are negligible. But just because it is easy to do doesn't mean that it is the right thing to do. Bona fide long-term investors should resist the temptation to overtrade. Usually you try to be so cute that you meet yourself coming around the revolving door and end up making a mistake.

Ignore the Rumors—Don't Buy Them

The old Wall Street adage is, "Buy on the rumor; sell on the news"—and this is just a way of saying that the market anticipates the news. But these days, information technology creates (and distorts) rumors so fast that they are not reliable ways to make trading decisions—and never were.

Cut Your Losses—Let Your Profits Run

Another old adage is, "Cut your losses, and let your profits run."

A successful investor isn't right all the time—just most of the time. Mistakes are inevitable. But you have to know what to do when you make a mistake. If you are correct 90 percent of the time but lose all your money during that other 10 percent, you're not a success. So the idea is to keep your mistakes limited. When you have a loss, recognize it and pull out as fast as possible.

You should be holding a stock for one reason only—to make money. So, if the stock goes against you, you've made a mistake. And most of the time, it's a better idea to sell the stock than to hold onto it and hope that you are going to be right in the long run. There is no law that says that if you sell the stock, you can't buy it back later.

Never Confuse Wisdom with a Bull Market

Just because you are making money doesn't mean you got everything right. So always thank Lady Luck just a bit, and don't let being right go to your head and let overconfidence affect your future decisions.

Don't Try to Catch the Exact Top or Bottom

There's an old Wall Street saying that goes something like this: "The most expensive eighths are the top eighth and the bottom eighth." What this means is that investors can spend so much time and effort trying to catch the exact top or bottom that they end up missing it entirely. Getting out near the top and getting in near the bottom works just fine in the long-term scheme of things—and as a technically savvy long-term investor that should be your goal.

Learn from Your Mistakes

Often you learn more from your mistakes than from your successes.

The real name of the game is to try not to make the same mistake twice. Unfortunately, the market keeps coming up with all sorts of new ways for you to make mistakes. I keep thinking after all these years, "By golly, I have finally made all the mistakes it's possible to make." And then the market comes up with yet another way to make one. The stock market is the most humbling thing human beings have ever invented.

Read a Good Book

Read *Reminiscences of a Stock Operator*. It is a fictionalized biography of Jesse Livermore, one of the great speculators. He made and lost fortunes several times in his life and ended his life by committing suicide in the men's room of the Sherry Netherlands Hotel in Manhattan. That book remains, to this day, the single best book on the psychology of speculation. The seventy-fifth anniversary edition with pictures is well worth buying, reading, and rereading—many times.

I also recommend getting at least one technical manual on how to make and analyze complex charts. (I have a few suggestions for you in the Appendix.) Read them as needed, but remember the two rules of chart making and analysis. The first is that the first 10 percent of the effort produces 90 percent of the results, and the second is to keep it simple: Having a complex chart with a whole assortment of indicators on it never gives that much better an answer than the basic chart I described in Chapter 6.

Instead of a complex chart, then, you are much better off with a basic long-term chart and an understanding of the general rules by which the market runs.

Backup, Backup, Backup

This is obvious advice, but an anecdote is in order here.

In 1979, when I was at Putnam, a fire wiped out the fifth floor, where the Market Analysis Department, Trading

Department, Bond Department, and a number of money managers had offices.

We had to sublet space next door while our offices were being rebuilt. I issued a memo during the recovery process that announced, "Due to circumstances beyond our control, for the immediate future, the Market Analysis Department will be called the 'charred room.'" (Say it out loud; it may help.)

But it was interesting, too, philosophically. The stuff we were working on got left on our desks. All the charts we looked at every day had been up on the wall. So everything that was important to our day-to-day operation was gone. All the stuff we didn't look at very much, though, was filed away in file drawers. It was a little crisp around the edges, but it was still perfectly usable. And we could look at that all we wanted.

So the trick is to keep the junk you're not using on your desk, and put everything you are using away in a fireproof desk drawer or file cabinet.

We all do just the opposite, though. We work on what's right on top of the desk. On our computers, we park our current files on our laptop, and we back up last years' work. But, if the ceiling leaks, it's gone. If the electrical outlet catches on fire, it's gone. To remind me, I have kept some twisted relics of things that were on my desk at Putnam when the fire started, melted by the heat into unusable forms.

So when you turn your computer off each night, make sure that all the stuff you are working on is backed up and locked away.

CHAPTER 24

"CALL ME LUCKY"

The Early Years

Technical analysts often have three characteristics in common: They are interested in numbers that change, they think visually, and they prefer cats to dogs.

I first got interested in the stock market when I was 11 years old and in grade school in Jamestown, Rhode Island. Numbers fascinated me, and I used to stop by the Kidder Peabody office in Newport to watch the ticker tape on my way home from the orthodontist. Later, when I went to Penn State, I used to hang out at the only brokerage office in State College—Green, Ellis and Anderson—to watch the ticker tape there.

The stock market crash of May 1962 really fueled my interest. The panic surrounding it was both dramatic and fascinating.

In those days, the stock market closed at 3:30 p.m., but one night the ticker ran until 8 o'clock because there was so much volume. The Dow Jones sunk from a little over 700 at the beginning of April to 525 in June, an unprecedented decline for those days.

Two of the three brokers at Green, Ellis had spotted the decline a mile away using technical analysis. This impressed me, and I got hooked on technical analysis.

One day I checked *A Strategy of Stock Market Timing for Maximum Profit*, by Joseph E. Granville, out of the Penn State library. (Granville is a famous early technician. Now in his eighties, he still publishes a market letter.) I carpooled back home to the Philadelphia area and read the book in the back seat of the car. The book absolutely fascinated me—a trip has never passed so quickly—and I started plotting and following a number of technical indicators immediately afterward. (I've discovered subsequently that quite a number of other market analysts who are about my age first got hooked on technical analysis by that very same book.)

Penn State didn't teach technical analysis, so in my senior year I sort of created my own curriculum. It helped that one of the Green, Ellis brokers, Dick Williams, also was an adjunct professor at Penn State. I worked my way into the honors program for business administration, where I did my honors thesis on leading economic indicators versus technical indicators as used by stock market forecasters.

Using FORTRAN (a now-antiquated computer programming language), I entered a bunch of leading economic indicators month by month, whether they were positive, negative, or neutral. Then I added a bunch of technical indicators and noted whether they were positive, negative, or neutral. And then I used Penn State's hulking old IBM 7074 that took up half of the ground floor of the Business Administration building to calculate what the stock market did afterward.

The result?

Technical indicators led the stock market. Leading economic indicators led the economy but were only coincident with the stock market. So I concluded that if you want to forecast the stock market you must use technical indicators, not leading economic indicators.

This bore out research by the National Bureau of Economic Research that showed that the stock market itself was a leading economic indicator, and in fact, it was then one of the two best leading economic indicators. (The other was housing starts.)

And everything that has followed was all because of Dick Williams, the adjunct professor at Penn State and technically savvy broker at Green, Ellis and Anderson. I knew it even then, too. I proudly gave him a bound copy of my honors thesis and inscribed it: "To Dick Williams—who bent the twig and inclined the tree."

After I graduated in 1963, I desperately wanted to find work as a technical analyst, but Wall Street didn't do much technical analysis, and the firms with technical departments weren't hiring.

I had one hope.

I'd been given a letter of introduction to the technical people at Walston & Co., one of the few firms with a bona fide technical department. So I hand carried that letter and my honors thesis to Edmund Tabell, head of the department. Edmund Tabell wasn't in that day, but his son Tony was. I walked in with my letter of introduction and my honors thesis, and Tony looked at me and said, "Oh, a thesis! Just put it over there on the credenza with the others." And I never got hired at Walston & Co.

(Tony, to this day, says this never happened, but I absolutely swear that it did. The story, though, has a happy ending: Tony later became one of my most important mentors, and we remain good friends to this day.)

The best job I could get on Wall Street was at Merrill Lynch—as a research department trainee. But Merrill had a wonderful technical department, and I was determined to join it. The department only had four employees, and the chief market analyst was Bob Farrell (the same Bob Farrell whose rules of investing you read in Chapter 3). The statistical assistant was young Arch Crawford, the technician/astrologer who puts out a market letter to this very day.

I will always be grateful to Archie. It was because of him that I got my first technical analysis job.

Archie was always threatening to quit. Almost every week, he would come in and say, "I'm going to quit, Bob." And Bob Farrell would say, "Fine, Arch. Where are the odd lots for yesterday?"

One Monday morning Archie came in and said, "Bob, I'm going to quit." And Bob said, "That's fine Arch, where are the odd lots?" And Archie said, "No, Bob, this time I really mean it. I'm leaving on Friday."

So Bob Farrell had to find somebody who could be trained in four days.

A number of people senior to me badly wanted Archie's job, but they had no background in technical analysis at all, and I was the only one who could be trained in four days. So I was picked to go to work for Bob Farrell in Merrill Lynch's technical department.

And that's how I became a full-time technical analyst in April of 1964.

Working for the Merrill Lynch technical department wasn't quite the glamour job I had envisioned. The department got little respect back then.

For instance, Merrill Lynch was running cartoon ads at the time, one of which seemed to ridicule technical analysis. The ad showed a gentleman sitting at a desk pouring over charts on graph paper with pencils, rulers, and a printing calculator strewn all over the desk. The caption was, "Come on Charlie, put those charts away." (I always wisecracked that right after that ad ran, Bob Farrell had his name legally changed from Charlie Farrell to Bob Farrell.)

Our offices were tiny and well hidden in back of the telephone switchboard area. We had more lost souls visiting us than actual visitors.

We also had very little published exposure.

Merrill Lynch's official position was that it wasn't going to put out any market forecasts. It was doing roughly 10 percent of the volume on the New York Stock Exchange (NYSE), so if the stock market did 6 million shares of volume, Merrill Lynch would have done 600,000 shares of buying and 600,000 shares of selling. Merrill Lynch was not about to tell half its customers that they were doing the wrong thing.

But what was a technical department to do if it couldn't forecast?

Merrill Lynch had two newswires; one was a general newswire (where the JFK assassination story ran), and the other was a managers-only newswire. Bob Farrell published a market comment on the managers-only newswire on Mondays and Thursdays. A banner at the top read, "For managers only. Not to be reproduced or distributed." So, of course, the managers then reproduced and distributed it because of popular demand in the office.

But officially there was no stock market forecast out of Merrill Lynch.

After working at Merrill Lynch for a while, I thought I knew everything and decided to look for greener pastures.

Gerry Tsai's Manhattan Fund—The Go-Go Years

I was doing point-and-figure charts by hand on every NYSE stock in those days. The plotting data came from a firm called Morgan, Rogers and Roberts, whose office was just a couple of blocks from Merrill Lynch. In the late afternoon, I walked over to pick up the price-change sheets, and if Morgan was running a little late, I would hang around and talk to the guy in charge, Ike Ameleh.

One day in January 1966, I told Ike that I was looking for another job. And Ike said, "Did you ever hear of Gerry Tsai?"

Indeed I had. Gerry had gotten quite a bit of publicity for running the first go-go/performance fund, the Fidelity Capital Fund, and there had been a very flattering feature article about him in *BusinessWeek* a couple of months before. Ike told me, "Gerry's moving to New York from Boston to start something called the Manhattan Fund. He called me yesterday and asked if I knew of any technicians who were looking for work."

So I interviewed with Gerry Tsai. He hired me for $8,100 per year, and I started working at the Manhattan Fund just as it went public.

Gerry had no idea how much money he'd be able to raise. The first prospectus was, I think, for $25 million. Then, as the demand grew, the fund filed for $100 million. Then it raised it to $200 million. The fund finally sold $270 million in the initial offering—the largest mutual fund public offering in history at the time.

When the fund thought that it was going to raise less than $100 million, the technical department was just a microfilm machine in Bob Edwards' office with microfilm tapes that had a daily and a weekly chart of every stock on the NYSE. When the offering crossed $100 million, the technical department expanded, I was hired, and I set up Manhattan Fund's technical department on the fly.

The basic stock charting service in 1966 was Trendline Daily Basis Stock Charts. The first day that Gerry got his $270 million to invest, he could only buy two stocks because of some technicality. (The stocks happened to be Polaroid and Pennsylvania Railroad.) The next day he started investing more money. He'd write down the stocks he was buying and the number of shares he wanted to buy on a big legal pad. He'd buy 25,000 shares of something, and then, if that order got filled, he'd buy maybe another 25,000 shares. By the end of the day, he'd managed to buy 25 or 30 stocks.

That first night I took a copy of Gerry's legal pad and the evening paper home and updated the charts of the stocks he had bought in my Trendline chart book so that the next day he would have updated charts (Figure 24-1).

Both the Manhattan Fund and its technical department expanded like crazy as the money kept pouring in.

Our offices were at 680 Fifth Avenue, and as we expanded, we grabbed more and more space on nearby floors in the same building. A telephone company installer named George worked constantly in our office stringing wires up and down elevator shafts and anywhere else he could to link our growing operations together. After a while, it looked like a string bomb had gone off.

Prior to us, our premises had been occupied by Canadian Javelin, a Canadian mining and exploration company with, shall we say, a somewhat shady reputation. One night, as George

---

Figure 24-1: Copy of the Legal Pad with the List of Stocks in Gerry Tsai's Handwriting.

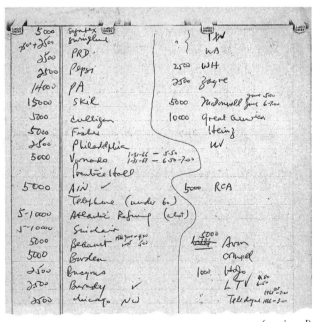

(*continued*)

(*continued*)

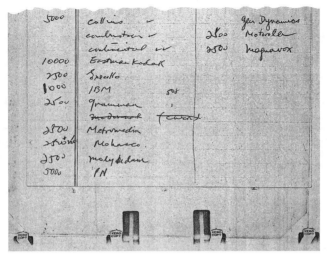

was rummaging around in the suspended ceiling trying to find a place to run still more phone wires, he pulled out a bunch of old mining maps.

I always wondered after that whether Canadian Javelin, whenever it wanted to announce a new discovery, just reached into the ceiling and pulled out a map.

Finally, we outgrew the building and moved to a single floor in a larger building at 245 Park Avenue.

Our technology, although up to the standards of the time, was ancient.

We had a ticker with a Trans Lux display. We had a Quotron quotation board that clicked and clacked. Our charts were drawn by hand. We had graph paper and Scotch tape. Typewriters. Mimeograph machines.

But we did end up getting one piece of state-of-the-art technology. We got 3- by 3-foot loose-leaf binders made that the manufacturer told us were the biggest loose-leaf binders they had ever made. We eventually found out that we had the biggest loose-leaf binders in the world.

For each stock in the portfolio, we made a one-point point-and-figure chart, a long-term point-and-figure chart, a daily chart, and a weekly chart. All four charts were displayed on two facing pages. Each chart was 8.5 by 11 inches, so we didn't have a lot of room left over. But we could look at four charts simultaneously.

This was what the state of the art was in those days.

We worked closely with legendary analyst Edson Gould, who was then at Arthur Wiesenberger. He worked for us on a retainer basis.

I went out for cocktails once with one of Edson's salesmen. He told me that Edson followed all sorts of things and, after a few rounds, he said that one of those things was the orbits of the moons of Mars. Well, astrology, then and now, is frowned on by market analysts. If you talk about the cyclicality of the moons of Mars, you will be thrown out of any investment meeting you are in. But if you talk about a cycle of, say, 62.8 days, everybody hangs on your every word as if you are one of the great wise men. So one of the greatest market analysts of all time, as it turned out, dabbled in astrology on the side—although for obvious reasons he never said so publicly. (I don't think the Market Technicians Association knows to this day that it gave one of its very first annual awards for lifetime achievement to an astrologer.)

We also followed an index that Edson Gould had made of seven big glamour growth stocks such as Polaroid, Burroughs, and Xerox that we calculated hourly and plotted along with the Dow Jones Industrial Average. We plotted the glamour average in red and the Dow Jones in black. We found that the glamour stocks led the market itself by a couple of hours—the red line always moved up and down a couple of hours ahead of the black line.

If there had been Dow Jones futures in those days, we would've made a fortune at Tsai Management. But there weren't, so we didn't.

It was an exciting time to be working in the markets.

In 1966, there was a bear market, when the Dow Jones went from 1,000 to 750. But then during 1967–1968 the Dow Jones went back to 1,000, and aggressive growth stocks performed fabulously well. It was a period of great speculation that ended up being called the "go-go years." The biggest go-go managers were known as the "Three Freds and a Gerry"— Fred Carr of the Enterprise Fund, Fred Mates, Fred Alger, and Gerry Tsai.

The Three Freds and a Gerry changed investing forever. Before that, people would buy stocks, put them away, and just hope that they would go up. But the Three Freds and a Gerry said, "We want to outperform the market." To do so, they traded more aggressively and calculated their performance day by day and week by week. They were the first to put performance guns to money managers' heads—all of whom are now cursed by the need to constantly outperform the market.

The Three Freds and a Gerry ended up inspiring so much activity that the American Stock Exchange (AMEX) ticker tape once ran 37 minutes late, and in 1969, the exchanges had to close one day a week, on Wednesdays, to let brokerage firms catch up with their paperwork.

It was volatile, but the volatility wasn't confined to the stock market. We were in the middle of the Vietnam War. President Johnson withdrew from the presidential race in March 1968. Racial desegregation was going on. There were marches on Washington. Martin Luther King and Robert Kennedy were assassinated. During the 1968 Chicago Democratic Convention, the Chicago police beat up students in the streets. The go-go years were part of all that. It was our biggest speculative mania since the 1920s and would remain the biggest until the technology bubble came along. For a very long time, in fact, I was able to go to client meetings with a copy of *The Go-Go Years*, by John Brooks, in hand and say, "I didn't just read about the go-go years, I was part of them." And I would open the book to page 147, where I am mentioned.

> "We keep everything," [said] Walter Deemer, a former Merrill Lynch analyst and boss of Information Central, who regards his charts the way an expert horticulturist might regard a bed of prize geraniums. "You may only want a certain graph once a year, but when you do, it's here."

After that was published, whenever somebody was fooling around in the chart room, Bob Edwards would yell to me,

"Watch out, Walter, they're messing with your geraniums again!"

So right up until the dot-com era, I could wave that book and tell people, "I have seen speculation—and this ain't it!"

Then, many years later, came the dot-com era, which, of course, swamped the go-go years in activity. But it took three decades for that late 1960's peak in speculation to be surpassed. And it probably will take another three or four decades before we see something like that amount of speculation again. Somewhere between 2030 and 2040, though, we will probably see another speculative binge. You can quote me on that.

It was at the Manhattan Fund that I was first introduced to hands-on computerized data processing. Tony Tabell installed a time-sharing terminal in my office that enabled me to tap into his data that were stored on a big Service Bureau Corporation computer—on a 110-baud connection. (Not megabaud, not kilobaud—baud.) As Tony explained it to me at lunch last year, "We were doing cloud computing way back in the 1960s."

Gerry eventually sold Tsai Management to CNA Financial, a big Chicago insurance company, for the then-staggering sum of $30 million. I remember vividly the day the announcement was made—it was the first evening that New York City closed the Central Park roadways to vehicular traffic, and two of my fellow junior officers and I were celebrating by taking a bike ride through Central Park. But as we rode our bikes through the strangely peaceful park, we realized that our ship had just sailed away, and we were still standing on the dock. We had no stock, we had no stock options. Senior management was going to make out like bandits, but we were nothing but bystanders.

Gerry Tsai was now working for CNA as its merger and acquisition (M&A) specialist, but he wasn't an M&A guy, and he did a couple of deals that almost bankrupted the company. The problem is that if you buy a stock and then don't like it, you can always sell it. If you buy a company and then don't like it, it's not quite so easy to get rid of it. (Gerry had always been a particularly volatile buyer and seller. One of the running jokes at Tsai Management had been, "Do you want to buy a Gerry Tsai doll? Wind it up and it dumps 50,000 shares of Sperry.")

After the merger, morale at Tsai Management went down quickly. All my friends started leaving. Also, the go-go years peaked at the end of 1968, so the market was going the wrong way. There were a lot of reasons for me to leave for greener pastures.

Putnam

The technical grapevine was very, very good in those days, and the word was out that Putnam was looking for a new technician. The company interviewed me and four others, and I quickly found out who the other four were.

Putnam gave a five-hour battery of tests, including psychological tests, to all job candidates. By today's standards, the tests were intrusive to the point of violating an applicant's constitutional rights. They also were silly.

Right after the tests, one of my fellow candidates called me up and fumed, "All I know is that they thought I was either a homosexual with heterosexual tendencies or a heterosexual with homosexual tendencies. And I haven't the slightest idea which."

Anyway, the tests so turned me off that when I flew to Boston to have my final interview, I didn't really want to work for Putnam and was kind of arrogant in my demands.

The interviewers laughed, assured me that the tests were nothing more than some sort of initiation rite, and hired me. The gentleman I'd be reporting to, John Bennett, knew Bob Farrell very well, and I had good references. So I went to work for Putnam (Figure 24-2).

After Tsai Management, Putnam seemed very conventional. It was much larger, of course, and much more established.

We had an Investment Department morning meeting; if a fund manager wanted to buy a stock, he had to make a presentation at the meeting. Then the analyst chimed in, and I also got to make a comment. So everyone knew what the thinking was. Similarly, if a fund manager wanted to sell a stock, he had to authorize the sale at the morning meeting, and the analyst had to put in her two cents. (This was a huge change from the state of anarchy in which Tsai Management operated. One day, for example, Bob Edwards was watching the tape, saw something, and picked up the phone to the trading desk: "It looks like someone's going to trade a block of Burroughs. I'd like to buy 10,000 shares on the cleanup."

"You're right," came the response. "They are going to trade a block of Burroughs, but you can't buy any of it—it's Gerry's block."

Bob disgustedly hung up the phone and muttered, "What's he know that I don't?")

Figure 24-2: Walter Deemer at Putnam.

Putnam
Vista Fund
Investment List
August 31, 1972

One of The Putnam Group
of Mutual Funds

Putnam also had a weekly Investment Department meeting where John Bennett would talk about the economic situation for 5 or 10 minutes, I would talk about the market's technical position for 5 or 10 minutes, and the bond people would talk about the bond market for 5 or 10 minutes. Finally, one of the analysts would do an industry review.

Attendance at these meetings was mandatory, which was very good for me. Even the people who didn't believe in technical analysis had to listen to me; I had a captive audience for 5 or 10 minutes every week.

My office was located right across the hall from the trading desk, which in those days had just three traders. Nowadays, of course, a trading desk has dozens and dozens of traders, but Putnam had just three traders and three clerical assistants at that time.

One incident that I witnessed in the Trading Department underscores how above-board Wall Street was in those days:

Mobile home stocks were the hottest group in the market in the early 1970s. Champion Home Builders, Putnam's favorite mobile home stock, went from a low of 5 in 1970 to over 100 in mid-1973. It then split five for one, bringing its price back to the low 20s.

Putnam's three aggressive growth funds owned a ton of mobile home stocks back then, and Wall Street knew it. It was thus a momentous occasion when Jerry Jordan, one of the aggressive fund managers, heard some bad news about Champion in the summer of 1973 and decided to sell a big chunk of his position. Jerry walked into the trading room, told Frank Mullin, the head trader, what was going on and told him how many shares he wanted to sell.

Back then, the two biggest brokerage houses that bid on blocks, Salomon Brothers and Goldman Sachs, were leery of speculative stocks such as Champion, so Frank immediately turned to the only player on Wall Street with big enough balls (as Frank put it) to step up to the plate on such stocks—Oppenheimer's Will Weinstein. He picked up the direct line to Oppenheimer.

"There's some bad news coming out on Champion, and I have a big block to sell. What will you give me for it?"

Standing behind him, Jerry was having fits. "Don't tell him that, Frank! He'll never make a good bid now!"

Frank turned around and gave Jerry an icy glare. "Look, I need Willy in the future. If we bag him on this, he'll remember it and never make us a good bid again. So I'm telling him what we know. He'll make me the best bid he can—and he'll be there for me again in the future."

So Willy made the bid (I think it was 18 3/4, down a couple of points from the last trade), worked his way out of the stock when it staged a feeble rebound—and was there to make more bids as Jerry and the other aggressive managers gradually sold all their mobile home stocks. (This was a shrewd move; Champion, which peaked at 26 in mid-1973, fell to 2 in 1974.)

Putnam's fund managers were wonderful, most of the time, but it was an article of faith among them that they could do no wrong. Ever. If ever a mistake was made, either the Technical Department or the Trading Department must be the culprit.

So the traders and I finally made a pact to give us each some relief—we'd take alternate weeks as the scapegoat. The first week, all the fund managers' problems were caused by the Trading Department. The next week, all the problems were caused by the Technical Department.

It worked well on the whole, but the fund managers took advantage of their immunity.

One of the fund managers, an especially vociferous tormentor of mine, told me that I'd done something wrong. I admitted that, yes, I had make a mistake—and as a matter of fact, the big boss had hauled me into his office that very morning and said, "Walter, you've been making a number of mistakes recently. If you keep this up, we're going to have to give you a fund to run."

That silenced my tormentor. But only briefly.

The problem is that because the stock market is so black and white, you know instantly whether or not you have made a mistake. If you buy a stock at 80 because you think it is going to 100 and instead it goes to 75, well, you may not agree with the 75 price, but that's where it is. So mistakes are all too visible and all too obvious. Since every human being is fallible, everybody made mistakes.

It was at Putnam, too, that I started doing intermarket analysis. John Bennett left Putnam in 1975, and after he left I started following anything and everything that influenced the stock market. The Bond Department, for example, was just down the hall from my office, and I wore a path out between my office, the stock quote machine in the hall, and the Telerate machine with all the interest-rate quotes in the Bond Department. Everyone does intermarket analysis now—but we were doing it at Putnam in 1975.

Putnam's administration was anywhere from okay to horrible. The administrators didn't manage money, which was what Putnam was all about, but they wanted to have control of the investment process. When I left, the Investment Policy Committee was comprised solely of administrators rather than the people actually managing money. It was like having a hospital's accounting department in charge of its emergency room's triage policies.

Also, I happen to be very outspoken, and I happen to have made a couple of enemies, including the big boss, Norton Reamer, who was . . . well, not everybody's favorite person.

In February 1980, I was invited to be a special guest on *Wall Street Week* (Figure 24-3).

The Monday morning after I appeared, one of the people who worked for me rode up in the elevator with Norton and said, "Didn't Walter do a wonderful job Friday night?"

"I didn't watch it," replied the manager of Putnam's entire investment operation.

My last crescendo of memos at Putnam occurred during the silver crisis in late March 1980.

Figure 24-3: Walter on *Wall Street Week* **between Marty Zweig and Lon Rukeyser.**

The Hunt brothers had driven up the price of silver, creating a bubble. Then, suddenly, the bubble burst, and silver sold off from $50 an ounce to $5 an ounce in a matter of weeks. The silver stocks collapsed, dragging the rest of the market down with them.

I was busy orchestrating a low because all the technical evidence said that we were headed toward one. I turned out reports day after day pointing out that we were getting closer and closer to a major low.

As the market cascaded down, the fund managers were eager to buy, but I thought it was too soon. So I put out a memo that said, "The opera ain't over until the fat lady sings." And then, as the market went down further and things were getting closer to a bottom, I put out another memo that said, "The fat lady is in the wings." Almost at the bottom, I put out a third memo that said, "The fat lady has come out on stage." And finally, "The fat lady is singing!"

I missed the bottom—the actual pinpoint of the bottom— by a day and a half. But that was great because remember, big institutional investors have to buy into weakness.

The day after the market bottomed, when I came into my office, I was told that, "Norton wants to see you right away." This was never a good thing. I went into his office, and Norton was quivering with rage, holding the prior day's trading summaries in his hand. And he said, "Did you see what those guys did yesterday?"

I quickly decided that the best thing for me to do was to quickly withdraw into my shell, so I just said, "No sir." And he said, "Do you know how much stock they bought yesterday?" "No sir." He said, "They bought 800,000 shares of stock yesterday."

That was about 10 percent of the volume on the NYSE—and it was the day of the bottom. And he yelled, "Do you know what that means? Those guys have never bought like that at the bottom before."

Two things flashed through my mind. The first was that it did not appear to be very good testimony to his investment leadership if he, the leader of the department, had never gotten them to buy at the bottom before. And the second was that I had given them the confidence to buy into cascading prices. I said to myself, my job is done.

I'd been at Putnam for 10 years by then. The fund managers loved me, but management thought of me as somewhat of a loose cannon. I always delivered an unhedged view of the market—but I hated playing politics, and politics were an important game at Putnam. So I decided to strike out on my own, and I did in July of 1980.

When I made my last presentation at the weekly department-wide meeting, the money managers gave me an ovation. I'm probably the only person who has ever left Putnam who got an ovation from the money managers. Norton tried to hurry the meeting along, but I still have very fond memories of that moment.

I left Putnam in July 1980 to form my own consulting firm, Deemer Technical Research.

The Putnam fund managers tried to hire me on a consulting basis—especially the advisory managers, who managed the private accounts, the pension fund accounts, the $10 million and up accounts. At first, they weren't allowed to (politics again), and then suddenly a couple of administrators left, including Norton, and they could, and I was hired by both the fund managers and the advisory managers.

I am delighted to say that since 1980, there have been no politics whatsoever in my professional career. I have been free to do what I thought was right. I simply follow the old Davy Crockett motto: "Be sure you're right, and then go ahead." I have no one else to think about.

That's luck in my book.

The Market Technicians Association (MTA)

The MTA was founded in 1972 by three people, Ralph Acampora, John Brooks, and John Greeley, who got together after work one night at one of the watering holes down near Wall Street and decided there should be some sort of professional organization for market technicians. Gradually, they set it up. It was called the *Market Technicians Association of New York*.

The MTA's goal was to have technical analysis more widely accepted. By far the biggest thing it accomplished in the early years was to lift the veil of secrecy surrounding technical analysis. Back then, "proprietary indicators" were commonplace; when someone came up with something, they kept it to themselves. The problem with that was not only didn't you know what was in their "black box," you also couldn't blend their "proprietary indicators" in with other things. The MTA, though, encouraged dissemination of methodologies. In that way, it broadened the expertise level of everyone because everyone knew what everyone else was doing. It was an unbelievably huge step forward.

The MTA was strictly a volunteer organization at first. During the early years, the big three technical departments in Boston—Fidelity, Wellington, and Putnam—sort of subsidized it. We ran the membership department at Putnam, Fidelity's Bill Doane edited and published the monthly newsletter, and Wellington's Bill DiIanni edited and published the quarterly professional journal. It was all done with volunteer labor and with the blessings of our respective firms.

I was the sixth president, the John Quincy Adams of the MTA. We were accepted as a splinter branch of the New York Society of Securities Analysts during my term. Before that, I'd tell people that I represented the MTA, which opened no doors whatsoever. But when I was able to say that the MTA was an associate group of the New York Society of Securities Analysts, we had instant professional recognition. During my term as president, for example, the Securities and Exchange Commission (SEC) proposed eliminating the collection and publication of member firm short-selling data, and technicians used that data quite extensively. As president of the MTA, I wrote a letter to the SEC urging it to reconsider. When the SEC found out that we were a splinter group of the New York Society of Security Analysts, the respect level went up exponentially.

The MTA's come a long, long way since those early days; it now has nearly 4,000 members and runs the highly successful Chartered Market Technician program. You can find out more about the MTA at www.mta.org.

There's also a technical analysts society strictly for professional technicians, the American Association of Professional Technical Analysts (AAPTA), which was founded in 2004. (I am a founding member.) The AAPTA is affiliated with the International Federation of Technical Analysis, and you can find out more about the AAPTA at www.aapta.com.

CHAPTER 25

THE FUTURE IS COMING

It's been said that navigating the stock market is like driving down a dark country road at night. You have a reasonably good idea of where you're going but can only see ahead of you as far as your headlights illuminate. As you proceed down the road, though, the path is lit up, bit by bit, as your headlights enable you to see further and further ahead.

As we proceed in our stock market adventures, then, the future will be revealed—but only bit by bit. In order for us to be able to share the journey, I've set up a forum on the web at www.walterdeemer.com/bookforum.htm where you, the reader, can ask questions of and discuss things with me as well as with each other. Even after 49 years on Wall Street, I'm still learning—and the forum is a place where we can all continue to learn together.

There are, alas, some questions that I fear are simply unanswerable at the moment. What are the ultimate consequences of the ultra-high-speed computerized trading that eventually will link all financial markets in every part of the globe together—every second of every day? How will the absence of specialists—the buyers of last resort—affect the market?

How will the growing popularity of exchange-traded funds (EFTs) affect mutual funds—and the markets in general? Will the Fed's recent intervention in the markets (QE and QE II) become more and more common in the future? And, from a more parochial standpoint, will these and other changes in the markets cause some—perhaps many—currently useful technical tools to stop working (as many did in 2008, to the chagrin of many analysts), and if so, can new ones like the National Association of Active Investment Managers survey (which earned its stripes at the October 2011 bottom) be developed to replace them?

The future, if nothing else, is going to be very, very interesting. Join us on the forum to journey down the road together—one headlight-length at a time.

SOURCES OF INFORMATION

(*Note:* Sources of information on the Internet are constantly changing. You can find an up-to-the-minute version of this list at http://www.walterdeemer.com/appendix.htm)

Free Internet Charting Sites

> Barchart.com: www.barchart.com/
> Bigcharts: http://bigcharts.marketwatch.com/
> StockCharts.com: http://stockcharts.com/

All three are very good, and which one you choose will depend on your individual preferences.

Free Internet Sources of Information

> Stocks at All-Time Highs: http://www2.barchart.com/ stocks/athigh.php

The source for stocks making new all-time highs we cited in Chapter 16.

DividendInvestor: http://www.dividendinvestor.com/

Dividend growth rates and yields are both available on this site. (Also see Telechart, below.)

Charts for Less Than a Dollar a Day

DecisionPoint.com: www.decisionpoint.com/

This invaluable site has many powerful features, including the ability to quickly plot a relative strength line against any other stock or index. Also available on the site: C plus the ability to see charts of Fidelity's 39 sector funds ranked by relative strength (a concept I have been using with considerable success for 25 years).

Telechart: www.tc2000.com/

For those who want to dig deeper into stock charting and do such things as rank stocks within a particular group or sector based on a very broad list of criteria (including dividend growth rates!). Worden gives you its highly regarded charting software free; you then pay for the data, as you would with any charting software package. (If you go to the site, you'll be greeted by a log-in screen; to get in, you'll have to create a free log-in by clicking on the "Create one now" button.)

The Chart Store: www.thechartstore.com/

This is *the* best source—by far—of historic reference charts for the stock market, the credit markets, the commodity markets, and the economy available to the general public.

Monitoring Sentiment for Less Than a Dollar a Day

SentimenTrader.com: www.sentimentrader.com/

If you want someone to monitor all the sentiment indicators for you, Jason Goepfert is your man.

Suggestions for Further Reading

Investor Psychology

Reminiscences of a Stock Operator, by Edwin Lefèvre, Wiley Investment Classics, Hoboken, NJ, © 2006.

Originally published in 1923, this is still *the* best book ever written on the psychology of investing.

Technical Analysis

Technical Analysis Explained, by Martin Pring, McGraw-Hill, New York, NY, © 2002.

If you want to dig deeper into technical analysis, this reference will let you dig as deeply as you want. It also discusses monetary indicators.

Technical Analysis: The Complete Resource For Financial Market Technicians by Charles Kirkpatrick and Julie Dahlquist, Pearson Education, Upper Saddle River, NJ, © 2006.

Another excellent reference on all things technical; it also has a brief discussion of monetary indicators.

Monetary Indicators

Money and Investment Profits, A. Hamilton Bolton, Dow-Jones-Irwin, Homewood, IL, © 1967.

The president of the highly-respected Bank Credit Analyst taught most of us how to use monetary indicators back in the 1960s.

The Kondratieff Wave

The Kondratieff Wave, James Shuman and David Rosenau, World Publishing, New York, NY, © 1974.

A good, readable discussion of the Kondratieff wave. There's also a lot of good information about the Kondratieff Wave on Wikipedia.

Investment Classics That Are Well Worth Reading (If You Can Find Them)

The Intelligent Chartist, John W. Schulz, WRSM Financial Service Corp., New York, NY, © 1962

The most intellectual discussion of and reasoning behind technical analysis ever written.

> *The Go-Go Years*, John Brooks, Weybright and Talley, New York, NY, © 1973

The best chronicle of the great speculative market of the late 1960s. (I make an appearance on page 147!)

> *The Money Managers*, Edited by Gilbert E. Kaplan and Chris Wells, Random House, New York, NY, © 1969

Profiles of 19 investment giants of the 1960s. One is the most accurate telling of the Gerry Tsai story ever written (and I told Chris Wells, the author, so when I saw him years later).

> "A Way Forward" by Dean LeBaron, Walter Deemer and Mark Ungewitter, Journal of Wealth Management, Vol. 12 No. 1. http://www.iijournals.com/doi/abs/10.3905/JWM.2009.12.1.010

This is an article I cowrote about long-term directional trends. The article explains recent trends from a historical perspective.

INDEX

Note: Boldface numbers indicate illustrations

Books of interest, 297–298

Boston Society of Security Analysts, 111

Bottoms, 67, 71–74, 143, 148–152, 153, 158, 266

   contrary opinion and, 77–78

   indicators of, 208–209

   head-and-shoulders, 152

   leading stocks in, 197–198

   selling climax and, 116–117, **117**

   shake-outs, 207–208

   testing the low and, 116–117, **117**

Breadth indicators, 163–164

Breadth thrust, 113. See also Breakaway momentum

Breakaway momentum, 113–116, **114**

Brean Murray, 25

Brokers, 11–12, 247–248

Brooks, John, 280, 291–292

Bubble markets, 55–56, 69–71, **70**, 101, 102, 118, 151, 192–193, 238–240, 280, 281, 289

   Japanese recession following, 212–213

   rolling, 238–240

   topping periods and, 144

Buffett, Warren, 21

Bull markets, 38, 55, 67–68, 71–72, 122, 184, 265–266

   bottom of, 67, 71–72

   breakaway momentum in, 113–116, **114**

   contrary opinion and, 77–78

   four-year cycles and extension of, 131–132

   head and shoulder tops and, 147–148

   irrational exuberance and, 55–56

   leading stocks in, 198–199

   oscillators and, 112–113

   secular, 98–99, **99**

   top of, 68–69

Bulletin board stocks, 202–203

Burroughs, 279, 283

Buy and hold, 7. See also Long-term investing

Buy signals, 66, 67–68, 265

   leading stocks and, 198–199

Call-put ratio, 168–169

Canadian Javelin, 277

Capitalism, 170

Carr, Fred, 279

Cash, 225–226

Cash-equivalent stocks, 201–202

"Cathedral of Charts," Fidelity Investments, 120–121, **121**

CD. See Certificates of deposit

Certificates of deposit (CD), 3, 9

Champion Home Builders, 285–286

Charts and charting, 81–93, **83**, 95–103, 259–260

   90/10 rule in, 82

   analysis of, 84–85

   basic, example of, 82–84, **83**

   constancy of data in, historic data and, 95–96

   Dow Jones Industrial Average, 96–98, **97**

   early, historic data in, 95–96

   Fidelity Investments and "cathedral" to, 120–121, **121**

   Generally Accepted Accounting Principles (GAAP) earnings in, 100–101, **100**

   inflation adjustment in, 103–104

   KISS rule in, 82

   least squares trend line in, 110

   log vs. arithmetic scales in, 96–98, **97**

   long-term, 95–103

   McDonald's example of, 86–91, **87**

   mean line in, 105–106, **106**

   momentum shown in, 83, 85

   moving average in, 82–83

ABOUT THE AUTHORS

Walter Deemer is a quasi-retired market analyst who worked for Merrill Lynch, Tsai Management and Research and the Putnam Funds before striking out on his own in 1980. He graduated from the Pennsylvania State University with honors in 1963 and has been aggressively continuing his education in the School of Hard Knocks ever since. He has been married to his wife, Bobbie, for 37 years, and they live on a still-unspoiled part of the North Fork in Port. St. Lucie, Florida, where they have identified 115 species of birds in their yard.

Susan Cragin is an English writing and composition instructor for the New Hampshire university system. Her last book, *Nuclear Nebraska*, dealt with the efforts of a small group of Nebraska ranchers to stop a nuclear waste dump from being placed near their ranches. Cragin is married to Mark Unge-witter, who with Walter Deemer and Dean LeBaron cowrote "A Way Forward" and appeared together as a panel during the 2010 Contrary Opinion Forum. Cragin graduated from the University of Connecticut and New York Law School, and attended the New York Art Students League. She lives in Concord, New Hampshire.